THE LAYMAN'S BIBLE COMMENTARY

THE LAYMAN'S BIBLE COMMENTARY
IN TWENTY-FIVE VOLUMES

THE LAYMAN'S
BIBLE COMMENTARY

Balmer H. Kelly, *Editor*

Donald G. Miller   *Associate Editors*   Arnold B. Rhodes

Dwight M. Chalmers, *Editor, John Knox Press*

VOLUME 15

THE BOOK OF
MICAH

THE BOOK OF
HABAKKUK

THE BOOK OF
NAHUM

THE BOOK OF
ZEPHANIAH

THE BOOK OF
HAGGAI

THE BOOK OF
ZECHARIAH

THE BOOK OF
MALACHI

James H. Gailey, Jr.

JOHN KNOX PRESS
ATLANTA, GEORGIA

10 9 8 7 6 5 4 3 2

Complete set: ISBN: 0-8042-3086-2
This volume: 0-8042-3075-7
Library of Congress Card Number: 59-10454
First paperback edition 1982
Printed in the United States of America
John Knox Press
Atlanta, Georgia 30365

PREFACE

THE LAYMAN'S BIBLE COMMENTARY is based on the conviction that the Bible has the Word of good news for the whole world. The Bible is not the property of a special group. It is not even the property and concern of the Church alone. It is given to the Church for its own life but also to bring God's offer of life to all mankind —wherever there are ears to hear and hearts to respond.

It is this point of view which binds the separate parts of the LAYMAN'S BIBLE COMMENTARY into a unity. There are many volumes and many writers, coming from varied backgrounds, as is the case with the Bible itself. But also as with the Bible there is a unity of purpose and of faith. The purpose is to clarify the situations and language of the Bible that it may be more and more fully understood. The faith is that in the Bible there is essentially one Word, one message of salvation, one gospel.

The LAYMAN'S BIBLE COMMENTARY is designed to be a concise non-technical guide for the layman in personal study of his own Bible. Therefore, no biblical text is printed along with the comment upon it. This commentary will have done its work precisely to the degree in which it moves its readers to take up the Bible for themselves.

The writers have used the Revised Standard Version of the Bible as their basic text. Occasionally they have differed from this translation. Where this is the case they have given their reasons. In the main, no attempt has been made either to justify the wording of the Revised Standard Version or to compare it with other translations.

The objective in this commentary is to provide the most helpful explanation of fundamental matters in simple, up-to-date terms. Exhaustive treatment of subjects has not been undertaken.

In our age knowledge of the Bible is perilously low. At the same time there are signs that many people are longing for help in getting such knowledge. Knowledge of and about the Bible is, of course, not enough. The grace of God and the work of the Holy Spirit are essential to the renewal of life through the Scriptures. It is in the happy confidence that the great hunger for the Word is a sign of God's grace already operating within men, and that the Spirit works most wonderfully where the Word is familiarly known, that this commentary has been written and published.

THE EDITORS AND
THE PUBLISHERS

THE BOOK OF

MICAH

INTRODUCTION

Micah and His Times

Only a few facts regarding the prophet Micah can be established with certainty: his name is an abbreviated form of Micaiah and means "Who is like the Lord?"; he was a native of Moresheth and lived during the period of Assyrian invasion of Palestine at the close of the eighth century B.C.; he preached a prophetic message dominated by a strong sense of social justice and directed particularly against the sins of the leaders in his time.

Moresheth, or Mareshah, was an otherwise insignificant place overlooking the Philistine plain and city of Gath, situated in the Shephelah, or lowland, between the Philistine plain and the mountains of Judah near Hebron. The village of Moresheth-gath mentioned in Micah 1:14 is now identified as a separate site about three miles north of Mareshah. During his earlier years the prophet Micah had observed the successive invasions by the Assyrians in the last part of the eighth century B.C. and the fall of Damascus to the Assyrians in 732 B.C., after the effort to promote a Syro-Ephraimite-Judean alliance against Assyria had collapsed during the reign of Ahaz. Then ten years later he saw the collapse of Samaria itself following an agonizing three-year siege of the city. During this period of crisis political alliances with Egypt had been futile, and Samaria's vacillating policies had failed to maintain her independence.

The decade following 722 B.C. was marked by uprisings in several Palestinian areas, centering particularly in Ashdod, the Philistine city nearest to Gath. Eventually (in 711 B.C.) Ashdod and Gath were captured by the Assyrians, and the former became the name of an Assyrian province situated right at Micah's doorstep.

In 701 B.C. the Assyrian advance finally came to the gates of Jerusalem, after the Judeans had succumbed to the temptation to stop sending tribute money about 705 B.C. (following the death of the Assyrian King Sargon). The reports of Sargon's successor, Sennacherib, agree substantially with those of the Bible (II Kings 18:13—19:36) regarding the capture of a number of the walled cities and towns of Judah and the unsuccessful siege of Jerusalem. If Micah lived to see it, his own town was probably incorporated into the Assyrian Empire at this time, to be returned to Judah later on. The price of independence for Jerusalem was again the payment of a heavy tribute to the Assyrians.

It is hardly to be doubted that Micah lived during the reigns of the three kings of Judah—Jotham (750-735 B.C.), Ahaz (735-715 B.C.), and Hezekiah (715-687 B.C.)—mentioned in the first verse of the book. That he actually prophesied during the reigns of all three kings has been questioned. Micah refers not to specific historical events but to conditions which existed for years, and therefore it is impossible to date his utterances exactly. Micah 1:6-7 seems to anticipate the fall of Samaria in 722 B.C., and may reasonably be placed before this event, but since the city was immediately resettled by the Assyrians, it may refer to a yet future destruction of the former Israelite capital. Micah 1:10-16 seems to belong to the period of the siege of Jerusalem and the devastation of Judah from 704-701 B.C., and it is to this period that Jeremiah's friends referred (Jer. 26:17-19) when, years later, they quoted the words of Micah (3:12). In general it has appeared reasonable to many students to date the chief prophecies of Micah in the period of the reign of King Hezekiah and more particularly in the period of active danger to the Jewish state from 704 to 701 B.C. But this conclusion is not fixed by unmistakable evidence. It is certain, however, that much of Micah's life was lived through a period of political crisis brought to focus periodically by the actual invasion of the Assyrian armies.

Equally significant for an understanding of Micah's prophecies is a glimpse of the economic and social conditions of his times. The eighth century was largely a period of prosperity for both Israel and Judah. Israel was particularly prosperous under Jeroboam II (786-746 B.C.), while Judah was also prosperous under Uzziah (approximately 783-742 B.C.). Foreign trade and international stability, together with the four decades of parallel reigns by Jeroboam and Uzziah, combined to ensure a marked increase in wealth for many of the people of both the Northern and the Southern Kingdoms. As will be seen, the primary message of Micah is an indictment like that of Amos against the abuses associated with this increase in wealth. Micah's message looks forward to the punishment of the people of Jerusalem and Judah, as Amos's had anticipated the downfall of Samaria and Israel.

The Authorship of the Prophecies of Latter Days

As the first three chapters of the Book of Micah and possibly most of chapter 6 are concerned with the immediate future of Judah and Jerusalem at the end of the eighth century, so the remainder of the book, chapters 4 and 5 and 7, is concerned with an indefinite future "in the latter days" when Zion will be restored after suffering in Babylon. If these passages are properly to be taken together, they are all addressed to the sort of tragic situation from which the godly man seeks deliverance in chapter 7. It is possible that this is the condition of the righteous poor of Micah's own time, but the reference to Babylon (4:10) looks too far into the future from the eighth century to be very helpful to Micah's contemporaries. References to the reassembling of the Remnant (4:6-7), to victory over assembled enemies (4:11-13), and to the calling up of leadership for the deliverance of the Remnant (5:2-6) presuppose conditions and events somewhat later than Micah's time, and sound like the anonymous prophecies found at the end of the Book of Zechariah (chs. 9-14). No clues as to the date of these prophecies can be relied upon, nor is it certain that they are all from one hand or from one point of view. In fact, two specific points of view may be detected in some of the material: on the one hand there are passages in which no human leader is evident, where it is the Lord himself who will accomplish the future blessing (as in Micah 4:1-4); on the other hand there are passages in which attention is centered on human leaders (as in Micah 5:2-4 and 5:5-9). The former generally reveal an interest in the triumph of God's purposes, while the latter stress Jewish political aspirations. The interpretation of these chapters must be undertaken, therefore, without a definite decision regarding authorship, date, or original setting. Each section must be treated as a unit and analyzed on the basis of its own language.

The Form and Content of the Book

It should be recognized at the outset that the Book of Micah is written in poetic form, showing the parallelism of thought which is even more characteristic of Hebrew poetry than rhyme and meter are of English poetry. The second of a typical pair of lines generally repeats the thought of the first in different words, sometimes expressing a contrasted idea, as in the first two lines of 3:4. At times more than two lines are linked in a chain of declarations with cumulative force upon a single idea, as at 1:7.

As this basic structural feature of Hebrew poetry is recognized, it becomes possible for the reader to see many identifications which the prophet does not make explicit in his writing, but which he assumes will be understood. In 1:5, for example, the names Jacob, Israel, and Samaria are identified and together are contrasted with Judah and Jerusalem—Northern Kingdom against Southern Kingdom.

Beyond the basic two-line verse, strophes or stanzas may be recognized in the work of Micah, corresponding to paragraphs in prose. The Revised Standard Version has separated these from one another with extra spaces, and it is to these longer literary units that the reader must turn for a clear understanding of the composition of Hebrew prophecy.

With Micah, larger unity and coherence are difficult to define. Chapters 1-3 express a continuing indictment of the people of Judah, particularly of the rich and powerful, and promise the evils of conquest as punishment. Chapters 4-5 look beyond the eighth century to "the latter days," when restoration to the favor of God will be brought about; the strophes or stanzas composing this section set forth the means of this restoration in expressions which are not entirely compatible with one another. Chapter 6 returns to the indictment of God's people, reviewing history in one stanza (6:3-5) and including the memorable definition of the requirements of the Lord (6:6-8). The final chapter is almost entirely a personal expression, like one of the individual laments of the Psalter, but it may be made up of fragments originally composed separately.

The Message of Micah

Micah stands as a perennial indictment of oppression and of leadership which makes itself strong at the expense of the poor and weak members of society. The book will never be popular with those who find it easy to take unfair advantage of their fellows, for it speaks of appropriate punishment for such behavior.

The Book of Micah, however, goes beyond the mere indictment of oppressive behavior to promise a future of blessedness and peace under God's instruction and protection. This blessing is not only for a remnant of Jews, but for many nations, particularly those who respond to the opportunity to join in peaceful worship of God. This ideal is coupled with the familiar and loved statement of the Lord's requirements of the individual, "to do justice, and to love kindness, and to walk humbly with your God." In the Book of Micah, the key to future blessedness is divine intervention, seen in part in terms of military victory, but seen also in the willingness of God to associate with the common man, as Shepherd of the flock (4:6 and 7:14-20) as in the days of old. On the whole the emphasis is on the quality of steadfast loyalty or "kindness" (6:8 and 7:18-20) both of God and of men. If this quality of faithfulness to the obligations inherent in the relationship between God and his people or among the people themselves is lacking, only disaster can be expected; if it is found between God and man and among men, then blessing may be anticipated.

The real message of Micah for all time is the stress laid upon the quality of loyalty to the obligations inherent in the relationship between persons. The oppression of the poor is simply a case of the collapse of the essential quality of faithfulness to obligations among the people of a community. Seen in terms of the unifying conception of relationship between persons, the book takes on a unity which transcends any possible diversity of authorship. Relationship between God and man is a sensitive and delicate association, granted by God's mercy and preserved through his instruction, but directly affected by the behavior of men, particularly their reciprocal behavior each with the other.

OUTLINE

God's Witness Against His People. Micah 1:1—3:12

Title (1:1)
The Forthcoming Visitation from God (1:2-16)
Common Sins and Their Punishment (2:1-13)
Sins of Leaders and Their Punishment (3:1-12)

God's Promises to His People. Micah 4:1—5:15

The Future of Zion (4:1—5:1)
Promises of Leadership and Purifying Activity (5:2-15)

God's Controversy with His People. Micah 6:1-16

The Summons (6:1-2)
A Review of the Case (6:3-5)
The Requirements of God (6:6-8)
Specific Indictment and Sentence (6:9-16)

The Distress and Hope of the Godly. Micah 7:1-20

The Momentary Triumph of Wickedness (7:1-7)
A Psalm Celebrating God's Mercies (7:8-20)

COMMENTARY

GOD'S WITNESS AGAINST HIS PEOPLE

Micah 1:1—3:12

Title (1:1)

Like other books containing the works of the prophets, the Book of Micah begins with a title, probably added by the editor who compiled the prophetic collection. In addition to identifying Micah as a native of Moresheth, the title mentions the kings of Judah during whose reigns the editor believed that Micah had prophesied.

The prophecies themselves are characterized as "The word of the LORD that came to Micah . . . which he saw concerning Samaria and Jerusalem." The utterances of most of the prophets are described as "the word of the LORD," pointing to the source of the inspiration from which they sprang. In connection with a number of prophetic utterances the editors used the word "saw," which has reference to the special visions or insight through which the word of the Lord came. The word is appropriate for the Book of Micah since the book begins with an imaginative scene, showing God in dramatic action (1:2-4), and includes the vision of the latter days (4:1-4).

Unlike the prophecies of Isaiah, which concern Judah and Jerusalem, the Book of Micah is described as "concerning Samaria and Jerusalem." Specific references to Samaria (1:5-6) and to its rulers (6:16) make this description appropriate.

The Forthcoming Visitation from God (1:2-16)

God's Coming and Its Meaning (1:2-9)

Micah's first prophetic word from the Lord begins with an invitation to all the peoples of the earth to listen while God presents his case against those who have disobeyed his will, particularly the people of Israel and Judah. Whereas verse 2 seems to indicate that the witness of God is against all of the peoples of the world, verse 5 makes it clear that he is especially concerned with Samaria and Jerusalem, the capitals of the two Hebrew kingdoms. As the message reaches its climax, it is Samaria to which attention is directed at first (1:6-7) and then Jerusalem (1:8-9).

In Micah's graphic prophecy figures of speech are not fixed; instead they shift as the prophet seeks language to express his thought. God appears first as a witness against the guilty. Then, as the prophet notes the place from which God arises to testify, he focuses on the "holy temple" which is God's dwelling. Finally, having thought of God's exalted dwelling place, the prophet visualizes God treading upon the "high places of the earth." The devastating effect of God's striding along the mountain peaks is represented by the prophet as the melting of the mountains and the splitting of the valleys, which break up and run like wax near a fire. The series of images directs attention in turn to God's sense of justice, to his holiness, and to his power. But throughout the series of figures the prophet emphasizes God's concern about human affairs: He is both a witness and one who comes from his holy place into the landscape of human history. Most commentators agree that the temple referred to is not an earthly building but the heavenly counterpart of the one built in Jerusalem, the one to which Isaiah's vision transported him (Isa. 6:1).

The significance of the visitation from God is not entirely clear from the initial invitation to the peoples of the earth, except that they are to hear the witness of one who has his dwelling in a holy place. Verse 5 returns to the witness from God; the entrance of God into human history is because of the sins of the Chosen People. Specific sins are not yet in evidence; the accusation is simply that both Israel and Judah have offended God. Offenses of two kinds are indicated in the terms used by the prophet: "transgression" indicates an abuse of privilege, the crossing of indicated limits for proper behavior; "sin" is the failure to attain a standard which has been set up for behavior, a falling short in achievement. Both by overextending themselves and by failing to reach indicated goals of behavior God's people have become liable to the prosecuting action of God. It is for this that he comes.

How will he proceed? Verses 6-7 sketch the intention of God with reference to Samaria. It will become "a heap in the open country," a tumble-down ruin, with its stones scattered into the valley, fit only for use as a vineyard. Its images, along with everything else, will be broken and burned. Its ill-gotten wealth, "the hire of a harlot," will be taken from the city and returned to those who made the city wealthy, and thence reused to prostitute some other city. It thus appears that the specific instrumentality of the destruction of Samaria, as the prophet saw it, was to be the peoples who surrounded it, the peoples from whom Samaria had learned her idolatrous ways.

A historical question faces the interpreter of this prophetic message: What was the status of Samaria at the time of Micah's words? At first glance the prophetic word seems to anticipate the fall of Samaria to the Assyrians in 722 B.C. But no complete destruction such as that pictured in these verses took place at that time. Rather, many believe that the message of Micah looks forward to a long period of slow destruction of the now defenseless city (after 722), carried on by Samaria's neighbors, her erstwhile lovers and patrons.

In two verses (1:8-9) which follow the initial message, the prophet speaks for himself, giving what he expects to be his reaction to the coming visitation from God. His words may be an explanation of a dramatic action such as prophets performed from time to time (see, for example, Isa. 8:1-4 and Jer. 19:1-13). What is clear is the application to Judah. The wound or blow with which Samaria has been smitten will reach Judah and Jerusalem itself. Whether verses 8-9 are contemporary with verses 6-7 is now of no great concern; Micah's message was directed primarily to the people of Judah, and particularly to Jerusalem. God's great visitation has to do with the sins of all his people.

The Coming Conquest of Judean Cities (1:10-16)

In a dirge which begins with the same words as David's lament over the death of Saul (II Sam. 1:20), Micah surveys the approaching tragedy of defeat at the hands of the Assyrians. Though not all the places he mentions can now be identified, his survey appears to include the western border of Judah, centering around the fortress and chariot city of Lachish, which took the brunt of the Assyrian invasion since it was on the border of Philistia. It was from this area that the Assyrians approached Jerusalem in 701 B.C.

Micah's lament is notable for the way in which he has expressed his message through a series of puns on the names of the various towns, the full effect of which is difficult to render into English. For those to whom "Beth-le-aphrah" meant "the house of dust," the command, "roll yourselves in the dust," had an immediate force, such as a reference to Los Angeles as the "city of lost angels" might have today.

To the ancient Hebrew the sober message underlying the word-play could hardly have been missed. Beginning with the memory of the ancient tragedy which David wished to keep from the Phi-listine enemy (II Sam. 1:20), through the dusty groveling, the nakedness and shame, the wailing and the anxious waiting, the prophet's words point to the tragic reality to be faced by Judah: "evil has come down from the LORD to the gate of Jerusalem." Lachish, the city of chariots and a regional fortress, may harness the horses, but in vain. Like a divorcee receiving a settlement, Moresheth-gath (a few miles north of Mareshah and Lachish) would receive "parting gifts" as she became the property of the Assyrians. Mareshah, accustomed to changing hands, would again belong to foreigners. And finally, like David hiding in the cave (I Sam. 22:1-2), the leaders ("the glory") of Israel would come to the border town of Adullam, fleeing from the conqueror. The prophet's survey goes full circle, rounding up the representative towns of the western section of Judah and returning to the recol-lection of the tragic times of David's distress as a parallel to the distress about to break upon the Judean state. Micah ends his dirge with the advice to parents to shave their heads in accordance with traditional mourning rites, because of the exile which awaits their children.

The prophet's survey of the approaching conquest of the Judean cities reaches its climax in verse 13 where he declares to Lachish, "You were the beginning of sin to the daughter of Zion." The path of conquest into the heart of Judah has been opened already by the entrance of sin into the heart of the state. Both paths center on the ancient fortress city of Lachish. In the same manner moral weakness in society today may serve as the path for future social and political downfall.

Common Sins and Their Punishment (2:1-13)

Woe to Planners of Wickedness (2:1-5)

Getting to particular charges of sin, Micah attacks those who "devise wickedness and work evil upon their beds!" In clear language (2:2) he explains the specific nature of the evil his con-temporaries planned as they lay awake at night, and in the con-cluding section of the strophe (2:3-5) he details the appropriate punishment now being devised by the Lord. As the rich and power-ful members of the community have successfully seized the properties of the weak, so now the Lord will raise up others (vs. 4) who will divide the fields.

In the evil time to come all the present haughtiness of such powerful members of the community will vanish, and instead there will be the old complaint of the ruined, "He is changing the status quo!" This time, however, the cry will be one of sarcasm and irony, as those who heretofore were ruined by the wealthy now watch the downfall of their oppressors and taunt them. Worst of all, those who have been high-handed in their evil deeds will end with "none to cast the line by lot in the assembly of the LORD." They will end by not having a share in the public decisions regarding the division of property; they will not even be represented by surviving members of their families.

Micah's poetic indictment of the planned—and perhaps technically legal—seizure of property by those in a position to accomplish the necessary manipulations finds a response through the ages in the hearts of those who have suffered economic injustice or who have watched helplessly while such injustice occurred. It stands as an assurance of God's concern for the weak, and of his intention to remedy the wrongs committed.

An Attack on Micah's Preaching (2:6-11)

In what appears to be the consequence of an interruption from members of his audience, Micah deals with objections to the kind of preaching he presented. The passage begins with a quotation of the interrupter's objection. Micah was asked to stop preaching about the evils of coming disgrace on the principle that to talk of such things is to invite them, or that those who are secure should not be disturbed in their "peace of mind." The opening word, "preach," is a contempt-loaded expression implying ecstatic or irresponsible utterance, "drivel," or even "foam." Accepting the slander, Micah apparently (a confused text here makes the point uncertain) hurled the term back into the teeth of his critics: "Thus they preach."

In a more reasonable spirit, Micah continues his answer to the interruption (vs. 7) with a series of questions addressed to those present. The term "house of Jacob" defines them as the ones called by God to be his people, but in fact questions the reality of their faithfulness in the present. Cleverly Micah turns from the interruption and continues quickly to present his charges of evil against the people.

In the three following questions (2:7-8) Micah raises the issue of the responsibility of God for the evil that is to come. Although he does not answer them, the form of his questions implies that the primary responsibility is upon those who have done the evil. The question regarding God's "Spirit" (here the inner being of God from which his moods arise) implies that it is certainly not impatience on God's part that is bringing an end to the security and prosperity of Judah. God would prefer to bring good rather than evil to his people, but their sins cannot be overlooked.

Micah returns to his indictment. The declarations of verse 8 are textually difficult, as the margin indicates. The conjectures show that the responsibility for the forthcoming evil is clearly laid upon the evil men of the Judean state, who have already allied themselves against their people, attacking their trusting fellow citizens as enemies. Like a conqueror they have driven women from their pleasant homes (vs. 9), and have robbed children of God's "glory." It is difficult to identify the implications of this deprivation, but apparently the wicked have, as it were, brought about a defeat of God himself, so that the children who survive will feel a sort of perpetual national humiliation, concerned more with religious feeling than with nationhood.

To these same wicked members of the community Micah addresses a final and emphatic dismissal in verse 10. It is a "goodby and good riddance" addressed prophetically to those who will be captives of the enemy, the opposite of Jeremiah's vision of the two baskets of figs, where the departing captives are viewed with some hope (Jer. 24:1-10).

In a final declaration (2:11), perhaps an independent fragment, Micah returns to the subject of preaching. Let a man begin to babble a lot of loose talk and lies, and the people will hail him as the kind of preacher they approve! He will be all the more acceptable if he announces as his subject, "I am for wine and whisky!" In this declaration Micah suggests the existence of the problem of intemperance in his day, and of the danger of any word of encouragement toward alcoholism. This is Micah's only adverse reference to wine and strong drink (compare 6:15 and 7:1). Evidently the rich of his day were too busy plotting serious economic sins to be attacked for indulgence in heavy drinking.

Return After Punishment (2:12-13)

In a brief interlude there comes a prophetic word which looks beyond the time of punishment to a time of restoration. Using the analogy of a shepherd leading his flock, a prophet, probably not Micah, describes the moment of departure of a noisy gathering of men from a place of confinement. The imagery is reasonably clear and its meaning can be determined to a certain extent: the fragmentary promise concerns "the remnant of Israel," which is evidently all that is left of the Chosen People descended from Jacob; this remnant is gathered into one place awaiting a journey or release; as it waits it is a noisy multitude, indicating a mood of joy rather than of distress. The king, who is the Lord himself and not either a descendant of David or a foreign conqueror, arrives to head the line of march. The actual beginning of the anticipated movement comes when "he who opens the breach" goes up before them. It is not clear whether this one who initiates the outward movement is to be understood as a leader (like a bellwether ram or goat) arising from within the gathering or as a chief shepherd who arrives on the scene to begin the day's move.

All details seem to point to an exilic setting. While it is not impossible that the fragment may refer to the release of the inhabitants of Jerusalem from their confinement in the city during the siege by Sennacherib in 701 B.C., it appears more likely that it belongs to the period in which the return from exile in Babylon was anticipated, and that it was inserted among Micah's prophecies to relieve their gloomy weight.

Whether it originally referred to the time of Hezekiah or to a later period, the passage is one further assurance of the intention of God to accomplish his purpose for Israel through a faithful remnant, whom he himself will lead. Such an assurance is unexpected in the midst of Micah's extended indictment of the sins of his time. But, like a good parent, God has often combined assurances of his love and of his good purpose with his reprimands and words of warning.

Sins of Leaders and Their Punishment (3:1-12)

When Leaders Oppress (3:1-4)

Micah's indictment turns to the leadership of his people, first to the "rulers of the house of Israel." Addressing them directly, Micah points to their special responsibility "to know justice." Not every member of the community can be considered responsible for knowing all the customary legal precedents (the term for "justice" is

often translated "judgment," in the sense of a decision handed
down in a precedent-making case). But rulers in positions of authority should certainly not "hate the good and love the evil." In
vigorous language Micah pictures the rulers of his people as the
Near Eastern equivalent of the butcher who prepares a slaughtered
animal for cooking and eating, and the people as the animal whose
skin is flayed and whose bones are broken and cracked and dropped
into the kettle to form the base for a soup.

The rulers, who have made the people cry in vain to God for
deliverance, will themselves cry in vain for deliverance (vs. 4).
"At that time," when God's visitation comes, he will not listen to
the pleas of those who have done evil.

When Prophets Mislead (3:5-8)

In his next indictment Micah turns to the prophets "who lead
my people astray." What he says implies that many of the popular prophets continued to be supported by the alms or generosity
of the people, as Elijah and Elisha were supported. Others, as we
know from Amos (7:14-15), were more independent financially
and refused to be identified with the groups of prophets abroad in
the land. Micah's accusation of his contemporaries, perhaps some
of the very same men repudiated by Amos, is that the tone of their
message depended on how well they had been fed. When they were
well received in a particular village, the message was one of
"Peace." When not so well received in another village, these unin-
spired prophets would announce the coming of a holy war against
its inhabitants, and thus attempt to "put the fear of God" into the
people. Either way, the false and misleading prophets ignored
the real problems of their times and paid no attention to the true
word from God.

The punishment designed for such men is appropriate: a complete eclipse of vision will come upon these prophets, seers, and
diviners, so that they will be disgraced and put to shame before
the people; they will then have "no answer from God." Micah's
word need not imply that they formerly had a message from God.
Rather, as they have been vocal in his name, in the day of their
disgrace they will be left without anything to say. The appropriateness of this fate is obvious.

On the other hand, Micah knows himself to be a true prophet,
filled with the power of the Spirit of God himself. In a rare auto-
biographical declaration he contrasts his own ministry with that

of the false prophets. The mark of validity in his preaching is the "justice and might" with which he declares the sins and transgressions of Jacob and Israel. What God directed him to preach made sense to a sensitive and right-thinking mind such as Micah's; his declarations were as consistent from town to town (if he actually preached throughout Judah) as legal decisions should have been. The message came to him with power from the Spirit of the Lord, and he expressed it before the people with vigor and assurance. To Micah, the man of sensitive conscience, the preaching of the false prophets lacked this power of consistent honesty. But his own preaching was faithful to the nature of God and to the consistency inherent in that nature.

When Only Money Talks (3:9-12)

In a third indictment Micah turns his attention to both religious and political leaders of his people, summing up his two previous indictments and emphasizing the basic evils of which all the leaders were guilty. Perversion of justice had been accomplished in part by violence and in part by bribery. Micah accuses the responsible leaders of both evils: they "build Zion with blood" and "its heads give judgment for a bribe." There is actual bribery of those responsible for judging—that is, the elders who meet in the city gate rather than formally appointed judges—and to these Micah adds the priests and the prophets. He has already charged the prophets with divining for money; now he accuses the priests of teaching "for hire."

Verse 11 links together the three directions in which an ancient Israelite might turn when he found himself in difficulty. If his difficulty was a wrong done him by a known member of the community, he might take his case before the elders ("heads") who sat regularly in the city gate; there presumably he might expect justice and award of damages from the guilty party. If the difficulty concerned his personal health or an injury in which the guilty person was not known, he might take his problem to the priest of the local shrine, who would solve it by referring to the ritual law or by the use of the sacred lot; or he could consult a seer or diviner, who would seek a direct answer from God.

Micah's indictment declares that a man without money would not be helped in any of these three ways. Only by bribing the judges or by paying the priest or prophet would he find any satisfaction. The prophet's concern is not simply that professional help should be available to the poorest people of the land, but that those members of the community with power and influence and knowledge of God's ways should put the proper exercise of their divinely given prerogatives above prices. In a day when almost every service has come to have a price tag, there is a real danger that qualities such as justice and truth and the nobility of disinterested public service may be lost to the community altogether.

The leaders of Micah's time were saying piously, "Is not the LORD in the the midst of us? No evil shall come upon us." On the contrary, says Micah, "because of you . . . Jerusalem shall become a heap of ruins, and the mountain of the house a wooded height." When the leaders of a people have turned so far from dependence upon the Lord as to consider the size of the reward they may expect instead of the rightness of a case, they are not in fact leaning upon the Lord, no matter how loudly they protest their trust in him. God, in turn, does not obligate himself to protect such leaders or the community of which they are a part. Micah foresaw the destruction of the Temple of Jerusalem in particular. Of what sacred institutions and monuments would a modern prophet speak?

GOD'S PROMISES TO HIS PEOPLE

Micah 4:1—5:15

The Future of Zion (4:1—5:1)

The Re-establishment of Zion (4:1-4)

In four familiar verses nearly parallel to Isaiah 2:2-4, and, like Zechariah 3:10, containing language similar to that of I Kings 4:25, there appears a vision of the restoration and future glory of Zion. In clearly defined steps attention is directed successively to the future exalted position of the Temple hill of Jerusalem, to the international reputation and importance of the Temple, and to the future peaceful condition of a world governed by the Lord of hosts. In figurative language the prophet sees the exaltation of the Temple hill above all other hills and mountains on earth; no geological upheaval is involved, only the social and political circumstances indicated in the rest of the vision. But the expected flow of peoples to the Temple must be understood as a literal expectation of the prophet. He foresaw a day when God's ways would be sought

out by many nations. "Law" (Torah, or instruction), the kind of
guidance expected from the priests in early days, would be found
in Zion, not just for restored Jews but for all peoples. The word
of the Lord would issue from Jerusalem. The prophet does not
think in terms of a written law, but of simple direct answers to
the problems of national leaders of the world. God will settle
problems between nations, whether near or far from Jerusalem.
The result will be that weapons of warfare will be of no value,
and will be made over into agricultural instruments, while people
will be able to relax under the shade of their own trees, enjoying
the fruits of these trees in peace, "and none shall make them
afraid." It is God's decree.

It is easy to see ways in which this vision of the future glory
of Zion follows logically the indictment of the latter part of chapter 3. True guidance from God, so rare in Micah's day, will become universal in the day envisioned. War and destruction, expected as punishment for the evils of the eighth century, will be
a thing of the past. Violence and bloodshed, the normal accompaniment of business life in Micah's day, will be replaced by a
truly peaceful existence.

It is rather generally agreed that the vision of restoration is the
work of a poet later than Micah, attached to the fragmentary
remnants of the work of the eighth-century prophet, as it has also
been inserted into the work of Isaiah (2:2-4). As such an addition to the work of Micah it corrects the impression of despair
left by the early prophet and sketches the glorious state of things
when the sufferings of the period of punishment will come to an
end. This addition belongs to the more theological of the two
groups of additions to the work of the original Micah, since it
stresses the judgment of God himself from Jerusalem. The passage declares God's intention for the world of "the latter days" in
a way that has not been surpassed. Details of the method of accomplishment of his will are not in sight, and thus the vision remains as an ideal, beckoning men of the twentieth century no less
than it has challenged the Jews and Christians of all ages.

The Dedication of the Faithful (4:5)

One verse stands alone following the vision of the future glory
of Zion. It brings things "back to earth" in a realistic statement of
toleration and of religious determination. Breathing an entirely
different spirit from the exalted vision of verses 1-4, verse 5 grap-

ples with present realities, in an age of increasing awareness of the variety of religious practices and beliefs. The writer of this verse was aware that the idealistic hope that many nations would come to Jerusalem seeking instruction from God would not be fulfilled immediately. If the returning exiles really expected an outstanding and world-attracting revelation from God as they set out upon the "second Exodus," they were disappointed; they had to recognize that Babylonians and Persians and the many other peoples around them would continue to follow the practices of their various religions. Only God's special intervention would change that: the returning Jews were powerless to bring all nations to worship their God.

But they could dedicate themselves to the Lord and determine to be faithful to him for ever and ever. While in Isaiah 2:5 the people are exhorted to "walk in the light of the LORD," in Micah 4:5 the determination to "walk in the name of the LORD" is expressed. By "walking in the name of" a god, the writer means simply that life and worship will acknowledge and honor only the appropriate national deity. No true Jew will become a worshiper of the gods of Babylon or adopt practices tolerated by these gods.

The Reign of the Lord from Zion (4:6-8)

This brief fragment continues to stress the divine presence and rule from Mount Zion, but centers attention on new details, with the result that the impression made is different from that of 4:1-4. Here the Lord is concerned with "the lame" and "those who have been driven away," apparently from among the Hebrew people. It is these weak and afflicted ones who will become the Remnant which in turn will be made into a strong nation. Zion is still central, now described as the "tower of the flock," but it is not the Temple that is important or religious instruction which is emphasized. In this prediction the goal is the return of "the former dominion . . . the kingdom of the daughter of Jerusalem," which may be understood as referring to the kingdom's greatest extent during the reigns of David and Solomon. From the extreme idealism of 4:1-4, which is essentially religious in its mood, the viewpoint has shifted toward the political. But here it is still God who rules; human shepherds do not yet appear as part of the picture. The practical problems of making the Kingdom of God real on earth are not within the scope of this fragment.

The Promise of Redemption (4:9-10)

Verses 9 and 10 interject questions addressed to the "daughter of Zion," and conclude with a promise of redemption by the hand of the Lord. The questions concern a time of distress for the people of Jerusalem, but they assume the presence of a king-counselor to whom the people should be turning in their fear. What that time is cannot be defined with certainty; the reference to Babylon, taken in connection with the reference to a king in Jerusalem, suggests the last days before the fall of Jerusalem to the Babylonians, either 597 or 587. At that time the kings, though still on the throne, were so ineffective that the people had reason to be seized with pangs like those of a woman about to give birth. The presence of these two verses, following the reference to the Lord's reign from Zion, may perhaps be attributed to a desire on the part of an editor to emphasize for his time the fact that God rules over Zion whether an earthly king is to be found there or not.

The announcement of the course of events following the fall of Jerusalem—residence in the open country and a journey to Babylon—is followed by the promise of rescue and redemption. It is the Lord who will accomplish the restoration of his people. Though originally intended for a time of despair and extreme political uncertainty, the concluding verse of this section is also appropriate for a time of overconfidence in the achievements of men.

The Fate of Zion's Enemies (4:11-13)

The next section deals with the enemies of Zion and, in a remarkably bloodthirsty mood, ascribes thoughts to the Lord remote from those of the vision of the nations seeking instruction in 4:1-4. This passage perhaps expresses an editor's idea of the way in which the Lord's redemption (not defined in 4:10) would take place. Nations which have assembled with the idea of the conquest of Zion learn to their sorrow that Zion is no weakling, but that she has horns and hoofs of metal and knows how to use the latter to beat out the grain from the sheaves gathered in harvest. The fate of the enemies of Zion, according to the picture presented in this brief fragment, will be for them to bring their wealth to the very gates of Zion as they prepare their hostile attack and then to have that wealth snatched from them by the victim they had come to rape.

It is difficult for modern men, conditioned by the ideals of Christianity and the exalted vision of Isaiah 40-55 and other parts of the Old Testament, to see how such thoughts can be ascribed to God. It must be remembered, of course, that such a fragment as this arose out of the deep distress of siege—such as that of 701 B.C. when Sennacherib nearly conquered Jerusalem or that of 485 B.C. when the Persians apparently put down an effort to establish a Davidic kingdom in Jerusalem. At such a time of dire need and extremity it is easier to ascribe ideas of vengeance to God than it is in more peaceful times. And it must be recalled that the Hebrew people had a strong sense of God's justice and power to accomplish his purpose. At times they believed that he would use natural forces to achieve his ends (as in the song of Deborah, Judges 5: 20-21), but they also believed that he made use of human instruments. Here the whole people of God serve to accomplish his punishment of the assembled enemies of his Chosen People. When modern man hesitates to ascribe thoughts of vengeance to God, he ends often by not ascribing to him any specific thoughts regarding individuals or nations. The Hebrew, on the other hand, had a vivid sense of God's concern for his people and developed in the postexilic period a strong feeling that all the wealth of the nations is really the property of "the Lord of the whole earth."

The Siege (5:1)

One obscure verse depicts the moment of defeat at the end of a siege. Whether the city concerned is Samaria (in 722 B.C.) or Jerusalem (as perhaps anticipated for 701 B.C. by Micah, or as actually realized in 587 B.C.) cannot be determined. The reference to the "ruler" or judge of Israel suggests the Northern Kingdom, though the term "Israel" may refer to what remained of the once united kingdom in later periods.

The verse serves as a transition from the sufferings of siege and defeat found in the latter part of chapter 4 to the topic of leadership with which chapter 5 will be concerned. In the transitional verse the people are in dire straits; they have not been able to "arise and thresh" their enemies. Instead their leader, here seen as one of the ancient judges, is powerless (like Samson?) to defend them against the foe.

Promises of Leadership and Purifying Activity (5:2-15)

The Leader from Bethlehem (5:2-4)

Having introduced the subject of leadership, to which he has not previously referred, the editor of the Book of Micah now inserts a fragment of prophecy regarding "one who is to be ruler in Israel." The fragment points to the origin of the expected ruler, and then indicates the nature of the leadership he will provide. Like the other fragments which make up this section of the book, it is not easy to date precisely, and its very ambiguity serves to make possible its attachment to more than one historical setting. (For its use in the New Testament see Matthew 2:6 and John 7:42.)

What is said is clear enough. Bethlehem of the district of Ephrathah, the home of Ruth's first husband (Ruth 4:11), is addressed as little among the clans of Judah and is told that a ruler for Israel will arise from her midst. This ruler is from ancient times; thus the fragment indicates the depth of the historical perspective, pointing to the time of the origins of the dynasty of David. In this ambiguous way the prophecy refers to the whole dynasty of David from David himself to the scion of the moment or of the future.

The moment of particular concern in the prophecy is a time of distress when the people as a whole are awaiting deliverance (thus is to be understood the figure of the woman in travail). A part of the people have become separated from the rest, and the end of the period of distress appears to coincide with an anticipated reunion of the separated brothers. Locating such a moment in Hebrew history with any certainty is not easy. The editor evidently considered that it referred to the time of Micah, and thus that it concerned the division between northern and southern tribes and a reunion which was possibly expected after the fall of Samaria during the distress under Assyrian pressure on Judah. It could almost as well apply to a return of exiles to Jerusalem. Or it may have originated even earlier in the period, when the line of David was reinstated on the throne of Jerusalem under Joash about 837 B.C.

Whatever the setting from which the prophecy actually arose, its important feature is the promise of leadership for the people. The Davidic ruler will arise to feed his flock, that is, to be their

leader in international and internal political life. Only through the
"strength of the LORD" and "in the majesty of the name of the
LORD his God" will he be able to accomplish his work of establish-
ing peace and security for his people. He is God's earthly deputy,
exalted to greatness because he represents God.

Prophecies such as this one formed the ground from which
arose the postexilic and pre-Christian Messianic hope. Originally
concerned with some specific historical situation from which deliverance by a great leader was expected, these prophecies came
to be reinterpreted for new crises, and ultimately they were understood as referring to a great Anointed Deliverer, the Messiah.

Here the accomplishment of deliverance is seen as the work of
a descendant of David who will serve his people as a shepherd,
strengthened by the power and name of the Lord. Out of the suffering of a period of distress, as a result of the leadership he will
provide, the people will come to security. Where the ancient Hebrew saw this security largely in terms of material blessing, the
New Testament would interpret it mainly as a spiritual blessing,
but for both the security would be the work of God's Anointed,
the good shepherd, now identified as Jesus of Nazareth.

Deliverance from Assyria (5:5-6)

In these two verses there appears a declaration regarding deliverance from Assyria under the leadership of "seven shepherds
and eight princes of men." Taken literally, "the Assyrian" would
refer to the invaders of Micah's time, but the term may be a later
cryptic name for "Persians." Neither the seven shepherds nor the
eight princes can be identified; the combination may simply represent a succession of family leaders. What is important is the declaration that deliverance from the invader will be accomplished
by leaders raised up in the midst of God's people.

As in the preceding section, the religious aspect of leadership
for the people of God is eclipsed by attention to the political and
practical side. It is the drawn swords of men leading the people
which are central. Almost inevitably when the prophets centered
attention on the practical question of how God would deliver
his people, they thought in terms of military victories under heroic
leaders. Thus was prepared the soil of the Messianic ideal which
led many of the people of Jesus' day to expect him to be a military leader against the Romans.

The Remnant Among the Nations (5:7-9)

A brief fragment centering around two figures of speech characterizes the remnant of Jacob as it exists scattered among the nations.

The Remnant will be like the dew and like showers. These come at God's command, and cannot be stopped by men—even if harvest is delayed or seed is not in the soil. The prophetic figure may easily be extended to suggest the fertilizing effect of the Remnant's presence among the nations or the quiet way in which the scattering of Jews throughout the world took place, but primary emphasis is on the will of God which sent the Remnant abroad among the nations.

Further, the Remnant will be like a lion among the other animals, both the wild and the domesticated. As the lion tears in pieces, "and there is none to deliver," so the Remnant, scattered among the nations, will triumph over all adversaries. Again the editor has centered on the means by which the vindication of God's people will take place, and has thus expressed the common desire for vengeance. The distant goal of a world at peace has receded into the background, and attention now centers on the obstacles in the way, and upon possible means of overcoming these obstacles.

A Christian may properly interpret the fragment to emphasize the natural quietness and the powerful effect of the Church scattered among the nations of the world. Both figures emphasize aspects of God's ways of working out his will.

Purification (5:10-15)

The final fragment of chapter 5 has very little connection with the rest of the chapter. If it has any connection it is with the end of the preceding section where the term "cut off" appears. Working from this link the editor uses the fragment to shift attention from the destruction of the enemies of the people of God to the purification of the people. The fragment he inserts at this point leads back to the original theme of Micah's work, God's controversy with his own people. The date of this fragment is exceedingly difficult to determine, and it may well be the work of Micah himself, though it lacks the social and moral note of the earlier chapters of the book and would thus represent a phase of Micah's prophetic work not otherwise recorded. The emphasis on removing idolatrous practices makes it appear to be earlier than the Exile.

Whatever the precise date of the fragment, its theme of purification is quite clear. In that expected, but here undefined, "day of the Lord" to which most of the prophetic books make some references, the Lord will cut off certain specific focal points of evil in the land: horses and chariots, cities and strongholds, sorceries (for sorcerers) and soothsayers, images and pillars, and the Asherim. The association of horses and chariots with idolatry (paralleled in Isa. 2:7) is enigmatic: are these associated directly with pagan sun worship (as in II Kings 23:11), or was the development of chariotry in Judah an economic and social burden resented by the lower classes? Or did the horses and chariots represent a sort of spiritualized idolatry like the modern dependence on large standing armies or the possession of world-dominating fleets of bombers or submarines armed with the weapons of mass extinction? Whatever the significance of the horses and chariots, the prophetic oracle anticipates their complete removal, along with the more conventional forms of idolatry current in the last century of Judah's independent existence.

In addition, an editor assures the readers of the fragment that all nations will likewise feel the wrath and vengeance of God for their disobedience (5:15). Purification must come to Judah, but it will also reach to all the nations. Of what elements of idolatry should modern nations be purified?

GOD'S CONTROVERSY WITH HIS PEOPLE

Micah 6:1-16

The Summons (6:1-2)

Whether the sixth chapter of the Book of Micah is composed of fragments compiled by an editor from various sources, or whether it is, as it appears to be, a continuous formal message by the prophet Micah, cannot be determined. The whole passage reminds us of the first chapter of Isaiah and of Samuel's accusations in I Samuel 12:6-18.

The summons invites the people of God to plead their case before the mountains and to hear while the Lord presents his side of the controversy. The "mountains" and "foundations of the earth" present a cosmic setting for the conduct of the case. In a setting as wide as the world itself the Lord appears, like an ancient Hebrew entering the broad place at the city gate with a call for the elders to assemble and hear his complaint against his neighbor.

A Review of the Case (6:3-5)

Having called for a hearing, the Lord continues with a review of his case against his people. The review touches only a brief part of the history relating to the period of the Exodus from Egypt, mentioning specifically only the incident when Balak, king of Moab, sought to employ Balaam to curse the Hebrews. (The full story is told in Numbers 22-24.) "What happened from Shittim to Gilgal" refers to experiences at the end of the wilderness wanderings, specifically the indulgence in heathen orgies dedicated to Baal of Peor (Numbers 25) before the rolling away of "the reproach of Egypt" in the circumcising of the Hebrews at Gilgal (Joshua 5:1-9).

The opening question of this section remains pertinent for all time. God has repeatedly and powerfully redeemed his people, not merely bringing them from Egypt, but preserving them in the face of the hostility of the Moabites (as an example); in return the people have perversely and repeatedly turned away to consort with the worshipers of other gods and to indulge in forbidden practices. Has God wearied his people? If so, how? Modern man may well ask if it is not he who has become tired of God. Why else his quest for causes, his exaltation of individual leaders or of all-powerful states or political parties? Why else his continual quest for meaning in life?

The Requirements of God (6:6-8)

Speaking now for the people, the prophet asks what sort of approach will meet God's approval. His language is drawn from the ritual of sacrifice, and, as the succeeding verses show clearly, deals with the basic question: "Under the circumstances, what is the appropriate sacrifice to present that the anger of God may be appeased?" Each question citing a specific sacrifice receives a negative answer. God is not interested in the quality of the sacrificial animal, nor in mere quantity. Nor is the supreme personal sacrifice of a man's first-born son the sort of thing to please God.

What God requires has been shown to the inquirer. The declaration of verse 8 is addressed to man as a member of the human race under the generic term for man (*adam*), not under the term which refers to the individual within the group. What is presented as the requirement of God has a wider application than to the Hebrew people, and does not rest for its validity upon the revelation of law at Sinai or elsewhere. Any man who would approach "the LORD" (this is the particular name of God as he was known to the Hebrew people) must come with justice, mercy, and humility. No religion can refuse at least lip service to the qualities suggested by the three terms, once their meaning is grasped. The "good" to be seen in these requirements is bound to have universal appeal.

Each term deserves attention. Justice covers the particular virtue which Micah stresses in chapters 2 and 3, and will again stress in verses 10-11. What God requires is the doing of what is right and fair between men. Justice involves the sense of a standard of right and equitable dealing between men, as simple as the filling of a measure of grain which is the basis of a transaction, the accurate weighing of quantities agreed upon, the punishment of those guilty of agreed-upon misdemeanors. The conception of justice does not rest upon the existence of a published code of laws, but upon the general sense of mankind that all should do what is "right," however this is defined. One who fails with respect to doing justly cannot consider that he is acceptable as a worshiper of the Lord.

The second requirement laid upon the one who would approach the Lord has traditionally been translated "mercy." In many places in the Revised Standard Version it is translated "steadfast love" (avoided here because of the preceding words "to love"). "Kindness" suggests sweet and gentle behavior, the *noblesse oblige* of the nineteenth-century code of the gentleman. The Hebrew word involves all these qualities and more. It means the fulfillment of the obligations which are inherent in a relationship, even when no laws cover that relationship. Husbands owe certain duties to wives, not because these are defined in a marriage contract, but because they are inherent in the common understanding and practice of the relationship. So also between parents and children, between a man and his domestic animals, between buyer and seller, and— how much more!—between man and God, many obligations are inherent without being defined by legal codes or negotiated agreement.

The final requirement turns from the duties which men owe primarily to one another to that duty men owe entirely to God. Man, if he is to approach God at all, must do so in humility, and having approached in humility, he must continue to walk in this spirit. Thus the Old Testament anticipates Paul's repeated declaration, "By grace you have been saved through faith" (Eph. 2:8), and emphasizes the dependence of man upon God. No sacrificial offering will serve to open the way to God; only God himself opens the way, and it is by God's kindness that man may have any sort of relationship with him—hence the necessity for walking humbly with God.

Specific Indictment and Sentence (6:9-16)

The final part of chapter 6 includes two elements, mingled in such a way that division into separate sections is impossible. The principal matter in the section is a continuation of the indictment of chapters 2 and 3, emphasizing the techniques and results of injustice which are found among the people: the "treasures of wickedness," the "wicked scales," the "bag of deceitful weights," and so on. Again the prophet refers to the fact that the same evils have been prevalent in the Northern Kingdom of Israel, under Omri and Ahab, and to the fact that the Southern Kingdom has followed its northern sister in crimes.

The language of the section is still the phraseology of accusation as this was developed in countless legal cases brought before the elders of Judean and Israelite towns at their seats in the gates of their communities. The text is obscure in verses 9 and 10, but the Revised Standard Version has followed conjectures made in the light of the ancient setting of legal cases.

Verses 14 and 15 and the end of verse 16 turn from accusation to the plaintiff's appeal for a verdict, or perhaps to the declaration of an actual verdict by the assembled court. Again, as in chapters 2 and 3, the punishment to be anticipated for the sins is appropriate. Those who have treasured up their ill-gotten wealth will not be satisfied with what they eat; they shall "put away, but not save," as in a time of monetary inflation; their agricultural pursuits will not bring any increase; worst of all, they will receive scorn and contempt and will be a desolation.

The climactic passage of the Book of Micah has been passed, and the prophet or his editor returns to the unpleasant task of making clear the specific sins of his time and what their punishment is to be. More modern forms of the same sins will no doubt receive modern forms of the same punishments.

THE DISTRESS AND HOPE OF THE GODLY

Micah 7:1-20

The Momentary Triumph of Wickedness (7:1-7)

The final chapter of the Book of Micah begins with a vivid picture of the momentary triumph of wicked men within the people of God, while the godly man waits for the hour of salvation. Many interpreters do not ascribe it to Micah, believing that it includes words and expressions normally found only in literature later than his time and that it does not reflect Micah's basic optimism.

Whether Micah or another prophet actually composed the statement, it is a thoroughly pessimistic view of the Jewish community. And whether the "I" of verse 1 represents the prophet or Zion is not of great concern. The viewpoint is that of the lonely but faithful good man who looks out upon a society that has become hopelessly bad. He represents the Remnant reduced to its last individual, a Zion in which the multitudes of believers have become unfaithful to their sacred obligations.

The initial figure of speech likens the community of God's people to a harvest field or vineyard which has been thoroughly stripped of all fruit. No godly men remain. Like rotten fruit littering the ground, all that can be seen are those princes and judges who insist on bribes and the "great man" who with a word indicates his evil desire. In such conditions the prophet notes that no one can be trusted, not even the members of one's family.

Bad as moral conditions are at this moment of spiritual extremity for the good man, he sees that "confusion is at hand" (vs. 4), and he resolves to wait for the salvation which God will provide. What parallels to the evils of the prophet's day may be noted in the present moment? How may the good man be saved from complete and hopeless pessimism?

A Psalm Celebrating God's Mercies (7:8-20)

The Book of Micah closes with a psalm which celebrates the mercies of God. It is composed of sections which may have had separate origins but now form a personal expression, continuing from the pessimistic and realistic tone of verses 1-7. Like many of the Psalms, this passage moves through the attitude of prayer and praise to an optimistic tone.

The Submission of a Repentant Sinner (7:8-10)

The psalm begins with an address to the enemy of the godly man. Strangely, this enemy is a woman—the personification of a hostile city or people rather than an individual. The enemy, thus personified, is told not to rejoice over the low estate of the godly, who is pictured as sitting in darkness. The period of darkness will shortly come to an end, and it will be the enemy who will be "trodden down like the mire of the streets."

In the meantime the speaker will bear the indignation of God, considering his judgment as due because of sins which the speaker has committed. Out of the darkness of the present evil moment, the speaker confidently expects to be brought forth to the light by the action of God himself.

The darkness of the present moment is apparently due to the hiddenness of God, for the enemy has asked scornfully, "Where is the LORD your God?" The presence of God is not apparent to the enemy, and the only indication which the speaker has of his presence is the assurance that the present evil is from God because of sin.

A Confident Meditation on God's Restoration (7:11-13)

In what appears to be a disconnected fragment the author (or editor) of the final chapter of the book looks toward that indefinite day when God's purposes will be accomplished. In its present setting "that day" refers to the day in which the godly man (or city) will gloat over the enemy of the preceding section.

The unsatisfactory condition of the walls of Jerusalem, the rebuilding of which was the focal point of ambition for postexilic Jewish nationalism, was the irritating core of the boil of religious dissatisfaction. Different solutions to the problem are projected by the postexilic Jews: in Zechariah 2:4-5 the prophet contemplates a city without walls; in Nehemiah 2-6 we find the practical approach of political strategy and allocation of responsibility for actual construction; at the end of Micah the prophet-poet simply looks forward to a far distant day when wall-rebuilding may be a reality along with other blessings.

In a meditative mood the writer lets his mind look forward to the extension of the boundaries of the Jewish state and to the return of the scattered Jews from all directions. East and west are represented by Assyria and Egypt respectively, and also by the two seas, the Persian Gulf and the Mediterranean. North and south are indicated by the mountains which stand in these directions.

But the land (the Land of Promise, not "the earth") will be desolate because of the sins committed earlier. "That day" does not include a complete transformation of nature, as it appears to do in Isaiah 49:8-13, 19-21. The vision of this portion of Micah is a limited one, but it breathes calm and hopeful confidence in God's restoring work.

A Dialogue with the Ancient Shepherd (7:14-15)

Turning from the mood of meditation the poem addresses God as Shepherd of his people (7:14). God is asked to bring his people out of the forest and let them feed in the fertile pastures of Bashan and Gilead as they had once done, during the days of the kingdom period. Again the point of view is that of the loneliness of the Exile or of the postexilic period.

In reply (7:15) God promises to show wonders as in the days of the Exodus.

Further Meditation: the Effect of God's Wonders (7:16-17)

Returning to the mood of meditation, the poet reflects on the effect which the sight of God's wonderful actions will have upon the nations of the world. Graphically, he sees them "lick the dust" in abject terror as they come out of their strongholds at the sight of God's powerful actions. So far has the picture changed from the darkness and distress of 7:8!

A Concluding Address to God (7:18-20)

In the final section of the poem God is again addressed, but now the stress is laid upon the greatest of his wonderful works, namely, the forgiveness of sins and his passing over transgression for the remnant of his people.

Again the language can hardly be earlier than the Exile, where the faithful Jew learned that God's punishments did not imply a complete casting away of his people. Because of God's profound dedication to steadfast love—that quality of faithfulness to fulfill obligations whether defined by law or contract or not at all—the exiled Jew came to a deep and persistent inner security in his relationship to God. If God demanded steadfast love of his people, he also showed steadfast love in relation to that people. Even the sins for which suffering had come upon the people did not mean the complete end of their relationship with God. Hence there arose the sure awareness that God would "again have compassion upon us" (7:19).

In the light of this profound assurance the poet-prophet could address God with the confident faith of the concluding verses of the Book of Micah. The faithfulness promised to Jacob and to Abraham would manifest itself in the forgiving of sins in the time of distress. What other religion offers so much today?

NAHUM

INTRODUCTION

The Book

The heart of the Book of Nahum is an extended ode (approximately chapters 2 and 3) celebrating the downfall of the city of Nineveh in a battle or series of battles vividly described. The exact limits of this poem are not easy to define because of the possibility that at least two of the verses of chapter 1 belong to it. The lengthy song of triumph over Nineveh is written in the peculiar rhythm of the ancient Hebrew dirge, here used as a taunt song against a fallen (or falling) enemy. Its mood is not that of most of the prophetic writings, which were usually concerned with the correction of moral evil within the Hebrew community. Instead, most of Nahum is concerned with the physical details of the last hours of the city of Nineveh before its collapse. With photographic realism the poet relishes each detail, and he challenges the citizens of the doomed city to escape their fate (3:5-17). In keeping with the character of the dirge and taunt song (another example is found in Isa. 47) the language is terse, the measure short, and the imagery vivid.

As the Book of Nahum has been transmitted to us, an introductory chapter of quite different poetic character prefaces the body of the work. Chapter 1 is written in a longer measure and, except for verses 11 and 14 (see comment on verse 9), makes no direct address to the enemies of the people of God. Even these two verses do not make any clear reference to Nineveh (as does 2:8), and they may be understood as referring to the Assyrian capital only by their association with the rest of the book.

The text of chapter 1 is badly preserved, and in its present form obscures what was apparently the original alphabetic poem used as a preface to the ode against Nineveh. It is a psalm like Psalms 111 and 145, both alphabetic poems by individuals in the praise of God, and celebrates the way of God's vengeance against his enemies. The device of beginning the verses with the successive letters of the alphabet is not generally reproduced in English translations but is familiar among the Psalms (compare also Psalms 9-10, 119, and others). Its purpose appears to have been to serve as a structure for the elaboration of a theme, and perhaps to help soloists remember the words during worship. If the purpose of aiding the memory was one of the reasons for using the acrostic form, it was not successful in the first chapter of Nahum. As they now stand, the limits of the poem and its text are obscure. It is, of course, possible that the editor of the material in the book adapted the alphabetic poem celebrating God's jealousy to serve as an introduction to the ode against Nineveh, thus providing something of a prophetic setting for the poem which is concerned so largely with the physical details of Nineveh's collapse.

The Poet and His Times

The poet Nahum is not described as a prophet in the title (1:1). He is identified in the first verse of the text as a native of Elkosh, a place that cannot be located satisfactorily. Efforts to locate it have placed it in at least three areas of the Middle East. One site is near the remains of ancient Nineveh itself, but this is not attested from any ancient source; Jerome identified an Elkosh in Galilee; and a recent commentator has suggested that Capernaum may be the "village of Nahum," but no clear evidence connecting the prophet with any of these sites can be seen. The most likely possibility is a site in the southwest of Judah, on the borders of the country once assigned to the tribe of Simeon.

Of Nahum nothing is known except what may be assumed from a careful reading of the book. Because of the vividness of references to Nineveh it has been guessed that Nahum was a descendant of the exiles from Israel who were settled among the Assyrians after 721 B.C., and that he may have witnessed the last days of Nineveh. The reference to Thebes (3:8) has led to the guess that Nahum had traveled in Egypt. Neither idea is more than a guess, and it is not improbable that the poet was a native of Judah who watched events in distant Assyria with the satisfaction which is natural for the oppressed when they see a bully given his due.

The exact moment of writing cannot be determined. Chapter 1 does not specify the adversaries concerned or indicate by historical references the moment of the anticipated cutting-off of God's enemies. Chapter 2 takes its standpoint in the midst of the fighting for Nineveh at the turning point of the battle. Although it sounds like an eyewitness account of the last hours of the city's life, nothing specifically identifies it as such, and it may well be the poetic creation of a prophet predicting the downfall of the hated capital city of Assyria. Chapter 3 (together with 2:13) looks forward to the downfall of Nineveh from a moment not too far from the end of the battle, but this viewpoint may have been assumed by the writer as a literary device. No details of the long poem are exact enough (to our knowledge) to require the assumption that he had received direct information from the defeated city.

The moment (or moments) at which the chapters were actually written may be anywhere from the sack of the Egyptian city of Thebes (663 B.C.), to which clear reference is made in 3:8-10, to shortly after the fall of Nineveh, which took place in August of the year 612 B.C. If the composition of the book was after the latter event, it was soon afterward, in the flush of triumph that spread over the Near Eastern world. If, as seems at least equally possible, the material was composed as a prediction, it was probably written after the death of Ashurbanipal, whose long reign began with the invasion of Egypt and continued in a series of wars with the peoples on the borders of his territories. The successors of Ashurbanipal proved to be weak and ineffective (as they are described in Nahum 3:18), and the coalition of Babylonians, Medes, and Scythians was successful in reducing the fortress of Nineveh and its outposts during a period of four years from 616 to 612 B.C.

In the two decades from the death of Ashurbanipal to the fall of Nineveh when the Assyrian Empire began to deteriorate, an opportunity for change presented itself in Judah. Josiah, who came to power about 640 B.C., dedicated himself to the restoration of the proper worship and service of God. The discovery of the "book of the law" in 621 B.C. profoundly influenced the future course of the development of Judaism, but nothing definitely related to the experiences of religious revival in Josiah's time appears in the Book of Nahum, and it is safe to conclude that the message of the prophet grew out of the broader experiences of his time in relation to the general conceptions of God held commonly by the people of Judah during the latter part of the seventh century before Christ.

The Significance of the Book and Its Importance

From the point of view of usefulness to the modern preacher or teacher of the Bible, the Book of Nahum offers real difficulty. Concerned as it is very largely with the downfall of a great pagan city of ancient times, written in the mood of triumph and rejoicing over the disaster that was to overtake Nineveh, it does not seem to offer much to the followers of One who said, "Love your enemies and pray for those who persecute you" (Matt. 5:44).

As literature the book is admittedly sublime. The characterizations of the confused officers and people (chs. 2-3) are worthy of a place in any collection of world literature. The expressions of bitter hostility ascribed to God and shared by the poet and his readers are magnificent and frightening. The occasional words of assurance to the people of Judah seem out of place in the midst of the torrent of malice against the enemies of God, but from the literary point of view they serve to sharpen an intended contrast between God's treatment of those who take refuge in him and those who oppose him. This literary gem in the midst of the Minor Prophets should not be overlooked.

But mere literary merit cannot justify the inclusion of a book in the Bible. The explanation for the presence of Nahum in Scripture is to be found in the Hebrew sense of the justice of the fall of Nineveh. Where a modern writer might reflect on the "poetic" justice of the downfall of a great and terrible enemy, using language appropriate to describe conditions during the agony accompanying that downfall, the ancient prophet reflected on the event as demonstration of God's rule. His language was appropriately borrowed from the conditions which could arise in the last days of the siege of any ancient city situated near a great river.

It is therefore the view of God's justice and his overwhelming power to accomplish his purpose that makes the book significant. Thus the first chapter is most significant from the point of view of the student interested in the contemporary relevance of the Bible. Chapter 1 asks (vs. 6), "Who can stand before his indignation?" The acrostic poem (1:2-10), uncertain as its text is, answers strongly that no one can. Chapters 2 and 3, the "long poem" detailing Nineveh's downfall, add the declaration that not even Nineveh can stand before his indignation and wrath.

The Book of Nahum offers the modern reader one of the many

opportunities found in the Minor Prophets to consider the currently unpopular aspect of God's character as a jealous God. As Nahum saw it, this quality led God to action against those who flouted his authority or who took pride in their ability to strike terror to the hearts of their neighbors, but it also promised relief from such oppression for all those who put their trust in him. For modern man, who has heard much of the relief promised those who trust in God, the Book of Nahum emphasizes the urgency of taking his requirements seriously. Graphically it pictures one way in which God has acted against those who deserved his indignation and anger.

OUTLINE

God the Avenger. Nahum 1:1-15

The Doom of Nineveh. Nahum 2:1—3:19

The Fall of the City (2:1-13)
A Taunting Dirge Over the City (3:1-19)

COMMENTARY

GOD THE AVENGER

Nahum 1:1-15

Title (1:1)

Like other books in the prophetic canon of the Old Testament the Book of Nahum begins with a title, which is probably not part of the original composition. The title in this case consists of two parts: one describes the composition as an "oracle" (literally, "burden") concerning Nineveh, and the other indicates that the book is "the vision of Nahum of Elkosh." The title points specifically to the prophetic elements in the book, which are found chiefly in the first chapter and in 3:5-6. As has been indicated, little is known of Nahum or of Elkosh (see Introduction).

Two Aspects of God's Character (1:2-3a)

The body of the book begins with what has been identified as an alphabetic acrostic poem, the limits of which are difficult to determine because of uncertainties in the text. It is reasonably clear, however, that it extends at least into the tenth verse. As it stands, the poem begins with a sixfold declaration about God (1:2-3a) which is somewhat separate from the remainder of the chapter. In form the declaration is like declarations of God's great mercy and faithfulness found in Exodus 34:6 (quoted in Num. 14:18) and in Psalms 103:8 and 145:8. The latter part of it borrows heavily from the language of these passages. It is, however, the aspect of God's jealousy and his spirit of vengefulness against his enemies which is emphasized in Nahum's words, rather than his mercy and patience. The latter qualities are only hinted at in the expression "slow to anger" found in verse 3. At the outset of the alphabetic psalm of praise the poet points up the two contrasting aspects of God's character as these are expressed on the one hand toward those who have opposed God and on the other toward those to whom God has chosen to show his mercy and kindness.

God's Way in Nature (1:3b-5)

The poem continues with a description of God's actions through the most destructive forces of nature known to man in ancient times. The clouds are occasioned by God's walking along the mountaintops, just as the progress of a traveler in Palestine may be seen from a distance because of the puffs of dust that rise from his feet. The poet ascribes to the Lord the fierce heat which dries up rivers—and even seas—and which makes the flowers of Bashan, Carmel, and Lebanon fade. All destructive forces are evidence of God in action, including those which affect the life of man.

The reference to God's rebuking the seas (1:4) does not connect naturally with the drying up of rivers and streams, except that both refer to waters. It appears that the rebuking of the sea refers obliquely to the crossing of the Red Sea in the Exodus, since the language of Psalm 106:9 uses the same word "rebuke" with specific reference to the Red Sea. But the principal emphasis of this section of the poem is on God's activity through what modern men would call natural forces. He has the power to do destructive things in the world.

God's Way Against His Enemies (1:6-11)

The next section of the poem deals mainly with God's activity against his enemies. The poet asks how anyone can stand before the indignation of God. When his wrath is poured out like fire or breaks rocks, it threatens the "full end" or complete destruction of anything in its way, particularly those who have opposed God. Recent editors of the text of Nahum have suggested several improvements. In verses 8 through 11 the Revised Standard Version incorporates several conjectures which improve the meaning, and the over-all effect of the passage is quite clear: God directs his power against those who attempt to plot against him. "Not . . . twice" will trouble rise against God from the same source (vs. 9, see margin) or will God have to act against his enemies (the same verse as translated on the basis of the Greek translation).

Although his primary concern is with God's vengeance against his adversaries, in verse 7 the poet declares that the Lord is a stronghold in the day of trouble, and that "he knows those who take refuge in him." The goodness of God is not developed in the Book of Nahum, but it is not ignored. The declaration of verse 7 is similar in form to those of verses 2 and 3, and like them may ultimately have arisen from some creedal declaration in the ancient ritual.

God's Commands (1:12-14)

In brief statements full of difficulties for the interpreter (1:12-13 and 1:14) the poet speaks prophetically, communicating God's will both with regard to his enemies and with regard to those who have been afflicted by them. The difficulties of the passage arise in part from obscurities in the text (note the number of footnotes in the Revised Standard Version), and in part they arise from the alternation of address to the enemies of God and to his afflicted faithful.

In view of the plotting against the Lord, to which reference has been made (1:11), it is God's decree that those, presumably the ones guilty of oppressing God's people, will be cut off no matter how strong they may be (1:12). God's command (1:14) directs that the names of his enemies be no longer perpetuated, that is, that no descendants shall survive, and that they themselves shall die and be buried. Further, images, graven and molten, will be cut off from the sacred temples of the enemies of God. Thus God's decree involves the destruction of all elements assumed to have lasting value by those who have opposed him.

In this interesting passage God attacks his enemies in regard to four of the aspects of life generally held to have the highest values: the possession of power, the continuation of life, the perpetuation of the family name through offspring, and the practice of religion. The false value-structure of those who set themselves against God —in Nahum's time as evidenced by the Assyrians—is clearly shown to be weak and impotent, as he who is supreme repudiates those who refuse to give him first honors. Like the Second Psalm, this passage in Nahum deals with those who rebel against the authority of God and details their fate.

On the other hand, unlike the Second Psalm, the decrees of the Lord as stated in Nahum do not deal clearly with the way in which God's will for the afflicted faithful will be accomplished. All that is said in Nahum is that afflictions will be ended, the yoke of the enemies will be removed, and their bonds will be burst asunder. Those who have taken refuge in God are thus assured of restoration to a more satisfactory life, but the manner of accomplishing this end is not indicated.

The Proclamation of Peace (1:15)

The final verse of chapter 1 (as numbered in the English versions) focuses on a herald of good news and the message which he will bring to Judah. In words like those of Isaiah 52:7 we are invited to look for the feet of the messenger of good news. The substance of the message is first epitomized in the word "peace," which to the Hebrew meant far more than the mere cessation of armed conflict. Peace referred to a person's health, to the welfare of the community which made for both health and prosperity of its citizens, and to an order of life gratefully accepted from superior powers, either divine or royal. A term with such breadth and depth of meaning could express the ideal conditions for which millions of people in our time are longing.

The specific words of the herald point to the recognition of "peace" through feasts and vows, and call upon Judah to enjoy the accustomed rituals of ordered life under God's blessing. Finally, the word of the herald assures that "the wicked" will never again come against Judah, since he has been completely cut off.

This verse (like vss. 12-13) addressed to the suffering people of Judah is in sharp contrast to its context, addressed to the enemies of God. Whatever its origin, it may be understood as an effort to bring to focus the good tidings inherent in the downfall of Nineveh. Couched as it seems to be in the language of ritual proclamation and with the reference to the keeping of feasts, it lends some credibility to the theory that Nahum was composed for use in the New Year's Festival of the year 612-611 B.C. after the fall of Nineveh. In any case the verses announcing good news to Judah fall between the opening poem and the long poem taunting the people of Nineveh, and serve to relieve the intensity of feeling in the two major poems of the book.

THE DOOM OF NINEVEH

Nahum 2:1—3:19

The Fall of the City (2:1-13)

The Alarm (2:1)

The beginning of the so-called "long poem" against the city of Nineveh cannot be determined with any degree of precision; to some students it includes verses 11 and 14 of chapter 1 (omitting verses 12, 13, and 15) but does not include 2:2. However, it is more satisfactory to consider that the poem directed against the city of Nineveh begins with the alarm sounded in 2:1. The poet begins in narrative style, telling of the arrival of "the shatterer" or "scatterer" who confronts the doomed city. Immediately he addresses the inhabitants of the city, calling them to arms, to watch and to brace themselves for the assault. No particular historical personage can be identified from the term "shatterer," and it is evident from the rest of the poem that the call to arms is ironical. The doom of the city is sure, but as a preliminary to the account of its last days, the poet echoes the voice of the watchman as he alerts the people to the danger. How often had such an alarm alerted the inhabitants of other cities to the approaching devastation from the Assyrians!

A Prophetic Explanation (2:2)

Verse 2, printed in parentheses in the Revised Standard Version, must be treated as an addition to the descriptive poem on Nineveh. Whether written by the original poet or added by an editor, it offers a prophetic explanation of the divine purpose in the downfall of Nineveh. Only here and at 2:13 and 3:5 is the name or person of the Lord brought into the course of the descriptive poem, and of these only the last-mentioned appears to be original with the first writing of the long poem. The declaration in verse 2 refers not to Judah or Jerusalem, but to Jacob and Israel, ordinarily the designations used for the Northern Kingdom (before the fall of Samaria in 722-721 B.C.) or for Judah after the Exile as the successor of the once united kingdom.

The parenthesis declares the restoration of the people, Jacob-Israel, using the term "majesty" as the text stands, or perhaps (with a slight change of the text) the figure of the "grapevine." The plunderers who have stripped and ruined the branches are clearly the people of Nineveh and the Assyrian armies, who are now about to meet their own doom.

The Color and Confusion of Defeat (2:3-9)

An exceedingly graphic section of the poem documents the mad scurrying of chariots, officers, and noncombatants in the streets of Nineveh and in surrounding areas during its last hours before defeat.

The poet pictures the response of the soldiers quartered in the doomed city, as they are roused to its defense in answer to the call to arms. He notes the bright colors of shields and garments, the flashes of sunlight (and of torches?) from well-kept weapons and chariots, the prancing of the horses, and the excited movement of chariots in all directions. The scarlet clothes (and possibly the red shields) may well be a reference to the Medes, who together with the Babylonians and the Scythians brought about the actual destruction of Nineveh. This is a spectacular battle, alive with color and vividly descriptive of the attackers.

The confusion belongs to the defeated. Weary, perhaps from night watches, the officers "stumble as they go" (2:5). Hastening to the wall, they see the movable shelter or "mantelet" protecting the besiegers set up against the walls. Inside the city a flood increases the confusion of the defenders as the dammed-up waters of the Tigris or of its tributary are released. An extrabiblical tradition regarding the fall of Nineveh refers to the disastrous effect of the flooding of the city, so it is probable that the enemies released the floodgates in order to increase the confusion and to destroy the city's supply of drinking water.

The poet turns to the movement of frightened refugees, moaning and beating their breasts, and looting along the way, as stores of treasures are opened and poured out in spite of efforts to preserve some measure of discipline. The "mistress" of verse 7 cannot be identified; the translation is, in fact, only a conjecture concerning the meaning of the Hebrew word.

The Desolation (2:10-12)

All that can be seen is "desolation and ruin." In a brief section the poet describes the anguish of the people of Nineveh, reflecting on the similarity of the defeated city to a den of lions which has been robbed of its security. The question, "Where is the lions' den . . .?" is the Hebrew idiom inquiring, "What has happened to the lions' den?" The obvious answer is that the lion will now no longer bring prey for the lionesses and the cubs to devour. So the conquests of Nineveh are at an end.

A Prophetic Word (2:13)

The final verse of the chapter, printed as prose in the Revised Standard Version but possibly to be considered as the introduction of a different meter into the poem, provides an explanation of the destruction of the city from the point of view of God and also announces a final disposition for the lion cubs, whose continued existence seems implied by the preceding section of the poem.

Uncompromisingly against violence and oppression, the Lord of justice has taken his stand against Nineveh. Therefore the chariots will be burned in smoke and even the "young lions" will be destroyed. The prey will be cut off and the voice of emissaries will no longer be heard. These latter expressions refer to the gathering of tribute for the Assyrian king; no longer will his representatives enter the various subject kingdoms and make rapacious demands.

The poet-prophet was right. Though a new king, Ashuruballit, attempted to establish a continuing Assyrian rule at Harran after the fall of Nineveh, and later at Carchemish, his efforts were doomed to failure. The remnants of Assyrian power were gathered up by the Babylonians within a few years.

A Taunting Dirge Over the City (3:1-19)

With the beginning of chapter 3 the tone of the long poem against Nineveh changes slightly from the descriptive poetry which is especially characteristic of 2:3-9 to a series of taunting and threatening expressions in which the full emotional reaction to the event is developed in a variety of ways.

The Price of Plunder (3:1-4)

In the first section of this chapter the poet-prophet makes no reference to God or to his ethical demands and laws, but by a skillful balancing of images he contrasts the accumulated store of evil within the city with the price now to be paid for that evil in "hosts of slain, heaps of corpses . . ." The words of the poet are emotionally freighted: those referring to the evil deeds of the Assyrians—"lies," "booty," "plunder," "harlotries"— are loaded with a sense of moral condemnation; those referring to the punishment inflicted on the "bloody city" are loaded with disgust. In this section the description of the motions of the battle is reduced to verses 2 and 3a, which are reminiscent of 2:3-9; emphasis is on the rightness of the punishment inflicted.

The Public Disgrace (3:5-7)

A brief word specifically from the Lord announces the coming of shame and disgrace as the accompaniment of defeat for the city of Nineveh. The Lord again declares (as at 2:13), "I am against you," and in the light of this opposition the Lord himself will treat Nineveh with the form of public disgrace meted out to adulteresses as a part of their punishment (see Jer. 13:22, 26; Ezek. 16:37; and perhaps Hosea 2:3, 10). Or the Lord proposes to treat the women of the conquered city in the way Assyrian soldiers had treated the women of cities they conquered. The purpose of this public exposure both for adulteresses and for Nineveh was to make all onlookers turn away and refuse to offer comfort.

It is not hard to visualize the scene in a Near Eastern town when the wronged husband led such a public exhibition of contempt and the bystanders joined in throwing filth upon the guilty woman, but it is somewhat difficult for spirits infused with Christian conceptions of mercy to see the appropriateness of the metaphor as a description of God's attitude and threat against a pagan city. It is important to realize that in this descriptive passage the prophet-poet stresses the rightness of real punishment for a city guilty of many crimes against its neighbors and of sins against standards of morality accepted even in those cruel days. God himself has been offended by Nineveh's evil deeds.

A Taunt Comparing Nineveh with Thebes (3:8-13)

Nineveh is now taunted as the poet compares her to the city of Thebes, which the Assyrians had sacked in 663 B.C. Addressing the city directly, the prophet reflects on that event and predicts that Nineveh, too, will be helpless in the day of her collapse, with outlying fortresses falling like the first-ripe figs and with the troops acting like women. In the same way Thebes fell, though protected —apparently—by the waters of the Nile and supported by Ethiopians, Libyans, and people from Put. How thoroughly Thebes was protected by the waters of the Nile and by its canals is not known, but the taunt is effective because the two great cities were comparable in importance in the ancient world.

The Futility of Resistance (3:14-17)

The next two divisions of the poem ironically urge the people of Nineveh to provide for resistance in the face of the inevitable

doom. They are urged to draw water, which is always the target
of enemy efforts to weaken the resistance of a city under siege,
to get into the brickyard to provide plenty of bricks for the repair
of defenses, and to be as numerous as the grasshopper and locust
or as their own merchants, so as to provide for the replacement of
fallen soldiers.

But all such efforts will be in vain. Workers will be cut off by
the sword where they work or caught in the fires of the doomed
and defeated city. And even though the population continues to
be as numerous as the locusts and grasshoppers, it will disappear
like the clouds of locusts which fly away with a change of the
wind or weather. Resistance will be utterly futile.

The Final Scattering (3:18-19)

The final section of the poem is addressed to the king of Assyria,
and at first seems to lament the ineffectiveness of Nineveh's leadership in the day of defeat. In the Old Testament shepherds regularly represent military leaders, generally royalty. In the last hours
of Nineveh, shepherds and nobles are asleep instead of vigorous
in defense of the city. With none to gather them, the people are
scattered like sheep upon a mountainside.

The king did not survive the downfall of the city. The final
verse refers not only to the king's personal condition but also to
the fate of the city and its people.

Standing as it were amid the ruins of the great city, the prophet
sums up his whole theme of satisfaction at the defeat and downfall of the city so long feared and so hated by the rest of the then
civilized world. All will rejoice, for all have felt the "unceasing
evil" of the Assyrian power. God's justice will have been accomplished.

THE BOOK OF

HABAKKUK

INTRODUCTION

The Book

The Book of Habakkuk may be divided very easily into three sections, corresponding to the three types of material of which it is composed. The first section (1:1—2:5) is in the form of a dialogue between a representative of the people of God and God himself; the second section (2:6-20) consists of a series of taunts or woes against evildoers, spoken by the prophet on behalf of the people afflicted by the misdeeds of the evildoers; the final section (3:1-19) is in the form of a psalm and consists of a review of God's mighty actions against the inhabited lands and a prayer for the renewal of his ancient work.

The unity of the book has been questioned, in part because of the variety of literary forms found in it, in part because of the inconsistency regarding the identity of the evildoers referred to in the several parts of the book. Did the same author write all three sections? We cannot answer with certainty, but we may discover a unity in the parts of the book as it now stands. Whether produced by one author or by editorial combination, the book now deals with the problem facing the prophet of God's afflicted people who sees the immediately projected action of God as inconsistent with the character of God as he has been understood. The unity of the book does not lie in singleness of actual authorship, or in a uniform treatment of the problem, or in a single historical setting of that problem. Rather it is in the actual nature of the problem, which is viewed in a variety of emotional moods ranging from doubt to faith and including righteous indignation. Differing historical manifestations of the one problem and differing efforts to deal with these may account for some of the difficulties found in the text of the book.

The Author

Of the man Habakkuk almost nothing can be said except what can be determined by a careful examination of the book. His name has been identified with an Assyrian garden plant, and it has been suggested that he may have been a captive living at Nineveh or at some other point in the Mesopotamian world, but for this guess no evidence exists except the name. Tradition (found in the title to the Greek version of the apocryphal book Bel and the Dragon) refers the story of Bel to the prophet "Hambakoum son of Jesus of the tribe of Levi." This suggests that the prophet was a priest, like his contemporary Jeremiah.

The book (or its core, in the dialogue with God in 1:2—2:5) reveals the man through the personal testament of a soul confronting God in the face of difficulties. Here the prophet appears as a person of high ethical sensitivity, capable of the same kind of graphic descriptive writing as that found in the latter two chapters of Nahum.

It appears that Habakkuk, like Nahum, played no significant part in the history of his time, but made his literary contribution to those few of his contemporaries who were close enough to hear him read or recite it. The circumstances of this first recitation and the extent of the recitation can no longer be defined.

The "Wicked" and the Setting of the Book

Something can be learned regarding the setting of the book from an examination of the question: Who are the wicked referred to in 1:4, 13, and elsewhere? A study of the several sections of the book suggests that at different points the wicked to whom the book refers are the oppressive wealthy class native to Judah during its last days and the emissaries of a foreign power during that same period. The reference to the Chaldeans (1:6) definitely identifies the foreign power about to be raised up by God to bring violence and oppression upon the Jews, and there is no sufficient reason to change this word in order to identify some other oppressive foreign power at a different period. The most likely moment from which a prophet might look forward to the coming of the Chaldeans is in the latter days of the Judean kingdom in the period of Jehoiakim's rule, between 609 and 597 B.C.

The problem is the apparent identification of the "wicked" with native Judean oppressors in 1:4 and 2:6-17, and their identification with the foreign invaders in 1:11, 17; 2:5, 8, and elsewhere. This problem is further complicated by the impression that many of the taunts of 2:6-19 have their setting in the later postexilic period and by the fact that this section of the book quotes from or is influenced by other prophetical books, particularly the postexilic Zechariah.

The original core of the book was evidently concerned not only with the problem posed by the coming of the Chaldeans, but also with the injustices perpetrated by leading Jews during the reign of Jehoiakim. The wicked, therefore, are both within the people of God and also outside, those outside being the instrument of God to deal with the ones within. To the prophet's complaints about this situation the divine oracles of 1:5-11 and 2:2-4 were addressed. Later, additions were made to the book as new manifestations of the problem were dealt with in new ways, by elaboration of the counsel to faithfulness in the presence of wickedness (2:5, if this is an addition), by expressions of threats against the wicked in the name of the holy Lord (2:6-20), and by the psalm of confidence in the avenging might of God (3:1-19). Each addition is made to the book in the confidence that it helps to meet the basic problem posed by the presence of moral evil in the divinely permitted actions of mankind.

The Interpretation of the Book

The additions to the original core of the book provide the first interpretation of the prophet's message. Out of new (or different) manifestations of the problem the editors of the book brought together available insights into the solution of the problem posed by Habakkuk's original complaint as stated in 1:13, "Why dost thou look on faithless men . . .?" But the problem of the prophet Habakkuk, like all profound theological and philosophical problems, refused to remain solved.

In the first and second centuries before Christ and continuing to about A.D. 70 a group of pious Jews, vexed with impure and oppressive leadership on the part of the priestly hierarchy in Jerusalem, retreated to the desert area of Judea, overlooking the Dead Sea, and there established a community at a point now known as Qumran. They looked out upon a world in which violence and oppression were widespread, both within the people of God and from foreign powers. The Hellenistic Seleucid rulers were in control of Palestine at the beginning of the second century B.C. Later, after the Hasmoneans (or Maccabees) became Hellenized and corrupted with power, the Idumeans and the Romans intervened in Judean affairs. At some time during this period an unknown member of the group composed a commentary on the first two chapters of Habakkuk. This commentary, or *pesher,* as it was called, is an attempt to discover in the words and phrases of the Book of Habakkuk a special insight into the events of the difficult times through which the Jewish people were passing during the last centuries before the Christian era. Identifying the evildoers of the book with his contemporaries, but using terms which authorities have interpreted differently, the unknown commentator found insight into the problems confronting him and encouragement to remain faithful to the commands of God no matter how long the time of trouble might be. For this unknown commentator at Qumran, Habakkuk's problem was his problem, and the practical solution was to await patiently what God would do.

In the first Christian century the Apostle Paul turned to Habakkuk's words in his presentation of the contrast between a righteousness which depends on the effort a person makes to obey God's law and a righteousness which is received as a gracious gift from God (Rom. 1:17; 3:21-22; Gal. 3:11; and Phil. 3:9, quoting or referring to Habakkuk 2:4). In Paul's use of the words of Habakkuk can be seen a radical transmutation of one of the central declarations of Habakkuk: the evildoers of the prophet become all men, including those who seek to obey God's law; faithfulness becomes belief involving personal commitment but stressing the acceptance of a free gift from God through Christ; the hope of a religious man in the midst of difficulties ceases to be a mere endurance of evil, but becomes the power of God which enables that man to be more than a conqueror through Christ. With the insight common to the early Christian Church, Paul saw that the problem of evil was a deeper problem than that which Habakkuk had seen, involving even the "righteous" (in Habakkuk's sense), and that Christ had dealt finally and effectively with the heart of this problem.

It was Luther's rediscovery of Paul's understanding of the solution to the problem of personal evil as expressed in the Letter to the Romans which brought about the beginning of the Reformation. So again the vision granted to Habakkuk became the means of grace for troubled souls.

The problem of the evildoer as opposed to the righteous remains a practical problem, even for those who have received the righteousness of God through faith in Christ. To such the Book of Habakkuk continues to offer the personal testimony of a troubled soul and the answering vision from God himself, a vision of a long-suffering God "of purer eyes than to behold evil," who came as "the Holy One from Mount Paran" for the salvation of his people.

OUTLINE

A Dialogue with God. Habakkuk 1:1—2:5

The Five Taunts. Habakkuk 2:6-20

The Psalm of Habakkuk. Habakkuk 3:1-19

COMMENTARY

A DIALOGUE WITH GOD

Habakkuk 1:1—2:5

Title (1:1)

Along with the other prophetic books and separate sections
within these books, the Book of Habakkuk has been given a title
by the editors of the prophetic canon of the Old Testament. This
title names the prophet and defines his prophetic work without
answering many of the questions which we should like to have
answered. All that is available is the mere name Habakkuk; no
setting for his work and no personal history of the prophet have
been passed on by the editors of the prophetic books.

Habakkuk's work is described as "the oracle of God which . . .
the prophet saw." The word "oracle" (the phrase "of God" has
been added in the English version) is literally "burden," a word
frequently used to describe the prophetic message. Though the
idea of an actual burden was a part of the prophet Jeremiah's understanding of his message (see Jer. 23:33-40), the term is generally a stereotyped expression added by an editor to characterize
the work of any prophet. In Habakkuk's case the word "burden"
would seem appropriate for the prophet's own complaint, but in
fact it is used to represent the divine message which the prophet
"saw" (another stereotyped expression) in answer to his complaint.

The Prophet's First Cry (1:2-4)

The prophet begins his complaint by addressing a series of questions to God (1:2-3a) and by describing briefly the situation in
which he finds himself (1:3b-4). In the complaints and descriptive
passages it is clear that he does not speak for himself alone, but as
a representative of a people oppressed and surrounded by the
wicked. Though the words for "wicked" and "righteous" are sin-
gular in the Hebrew, the Revised Standard Version is correct in
reading them as collectives, involving groups of people in both
cases. The use of such collective expressions is common throughout the Old Testament.

Speaking for the oppressed among his people, the prophet asks how long his call for help will go unanswered and why he must continue to see violence and trouble with no one to deliver the victims. Strife and contention arise before his eyes, and worst of all, "the law is slacked" and justice does not issue as the end of the various legal contentions. Instead, "the wicked surround the righteous," and the cases they institute are wrongly decided for their own benefit.

At this point conditions under Jehoiakim may be reflected in the prophet's words. The "wicked," then, would be the princes and the king himself, against whom Jeremiah raised his voice (Jer. 25:1-27). The "violence," the "strife and contention," are within Judah. The "law" is God's law, perhaps that which had recently been rediscovered in the time of Josiah (II Kings 22-23) and which is generally recognized to have been Deuteronomy or a major part of it. Some sort of reaction against the reforms of Josiah must have taken place during the reign of Jehoiakim to provoke the language of Jeremiah and the questions of Habakkuk. But the language of Habakkuk is not so specific as to prevent its application to many similar situations when the just order of a society is perverted by a wicked leadership. For every such time Habakkuk voices the perplexity of the faithful.

The Oracle Concerning the Chaldeans (1:5-11)

In response to the prophet's complaint there comes an oracle from God which directs the prophet to look beyond the borders of his people at the astounding work which God is doing. It is to this section and to the second oracle that the title of the book, "oracle" or burden, properly belongs, though it may be noted that the arousing of the Chaldeans is nowhere specifically said to concern the people of Judah or to provide for the punishment of sins committed by the people of God. The oracle provides a descriptive interpretation of the events of the time before the Chaldeans actually invaded Palestine. It is the declaration of verse 6, "For lo, I am rousing the Chaldeans," which makes clear the prophetic character of the passage.

The projected work of the Lord is a thing which would not be believed; it is something to be wondered at. The verbs (as in Isa. 53:1) suggest the astonishment and near disbelief of people unprepared for the sort of work being accomplished by God. As the remainder of the passage indicates, it is the character of the Chal-

deans, not only the fact that God rouses them, that is the occasion for astonishment.

The Chaldeans are described in unique language as "that bitter
and hasty nation." Though they were probably no more fierce
than the Assyrians, whom they succeeded as masters of the world,
the rapidity with which they built their empire makes the latter
word appropriate. It is to their swift action in conquering the
world in a short period of time that the figures of verses 8-10 refer. In poetic language the prophet endows their horses with fan-
tastic capabilities.

The terror provoked by the aroused Chaldeans is suggested in
verses 7, 9, 10, and 11. Together these verses give the impression
that the Chaldeans acknowledged no law but their own, and that
they worshiped their own strength. The descriptive expression
"guilty men" of verse 11 is an effort to make the best of a difficult
Hebrew text. The description of a terrifyingly swift conqueror,
who has no particular concern for the rights of the conquered, is
clear from the passage. It is this character of the Chaldeans, whom
God is arousing, which is to astound the onlooker. As with Jeremiah, evil appears within the people and around the people. With
Habakkuk, however, the oracle declares that the rousing of the
bitter and hasty nation is performed by God himself.

The Second Complaint (1:12-17)

Speaking for the people a second time, the prophet addresses
God with a further complaint. In it he appeals to the being and
character of God, and from this perspective he reviews the circumstances which God seems now to be permitting, asking why
God does not end the injustice.

The second complaint begins with a question which affirms belief in the distinctive existence of God. The initial question looks
back to the existence of God as early as the mind of man can
reach. The expression, "We shall not die," is one of the so-called
"corrections of the scribes." The original Hebrew of this phrase
would have been "Thou shalt not die," a proper affirmation of
God's continued existence. Early scribes, however, felt that even
this affirmation implied some doubt, so they changed it to the in-
nocuous reading of the text. The prophet further characterizes
God as "my Holy One" and in verse 13 refers to his purity. God,
he alleges, cannot look upon wrong.

The second half of verse 12 addresses God as "Lord" and as "Rock," declaring that he has ordained "them" as a judgment and for chastisement. Some commentators have argued that this descriptive statement belongs properly to one of the oracles and not to the complaint, since it provides a clue to the purpose of the arousing of the Chaldeans. But such an interpretation does not in fact deal with the heart of the problem which engaged the attention of Habakkuk. The prophet and his people would no doubt have welcomed the punishment of the wicked oppressors of the poor among the people of Judah, assured that God had arranged for it, for they understood God's character as a righteous judge. But the problem of Habakkuk is clearly expressed in verse 13, and in the light of the conception of God who provides for judgment and chastisement as expressed in the latter part of verse 12, the problem is all the more pointed. How can the God of righteous judgment and chastisement permit the wicked and the faithless to swallow up "the man more righteous than he"? The prophet speaks for the relatively innocent victims of Judean oppression faced with the prospect of sharing the chastisement of their oppressors. And thus he speaks for the humble victims of man's inhumanity to man in all ages.

In verse 14 the prophet continues to address the Lord, but from this point onward he directs his attention more specifically to the situation in which his people find themselves. His description of that situation is entirely figurative to the end of the complaint. In the first place, he complains to God that men have been reduced to the leaderless condition of the fish of the sea and of crawling things. Instead of being rulers of the lower forms of life as they were intended to be (compare Gen. 1:26, 28 and Ps. 8:5-8), men are now disorganized and are the victims of the rapacity of the wicked.

Habakkuk's references to the "net" and "seine" (it has been suggested that the "hook" is an addition) are apparently a description of the grasping tyranny of the Chaldeans and of the luxury in which they lived as a result of their conquests. (See a similar reference in Jeremiah 16:16-18.)

The reference to sacrifices to the net and the burning of incense to the seine (1:16) has been understood as figurative language for a cult of military weapons or of the war gods Marduk, Adad, and Ishtar. It is the idolatry of the wicked and their blatant opposition to the Lord which disturbed Habakkuk. Can God let this go on

forever? The prophetic complaint speaks for the relatively innocent victims of oppression and of warfare.

Preparation for the Lord's Answer (2:1)

In response to the second complaint comes a vision for the
prophet to record (2:2-5) after he has announced that he is station-
ing himself as a lookout "on the tower" (2:1) to see what answer
he may have concerning his complaint.

Whether Habakkuk's words indicate his own decision at this
point to seek a revelation from God at a particular tower (of the
Temple?), or whether they provide the setting for the composition
of the whole episode of complaints and revelatory oracles, can
only be conjectured. The expression "what I will answer concerning my complaint" raises another problem: Is the "I" an indication of the prophet's representative character as spokesman for the
people of God and as spokesman for God to the people, and
hence of a mediatorial role, or is it a mistake in the text for which
only the Syriac translation provides the correct reading, "He will
answer"? The question cannot be answered with certainty, and it
is actually of small concern.

The Lord's Answer (2:2-3)

The Lord's answer begins by directing the prophet to write the
vision plainly upon tablets, "so he may run who reads it." We are
given no indication of the nature of the tablets, whether of wood,
stone, or clay, or of the size of the writings. What is important is
that the vision be easily read and understood, and that it be preserved to the certain time of fulfillment. The full significance of
the reader's running and the timing of the fulfillment are difficult
to discover. Either the vision is to be such as will send the reader
on the run toward the hastening fulfillment, or, as many commentators prefer, the vision is to be so clearly read—like a bill-
board—that even a runner may read it without pausing. The vision is also one that awaits its time, hastening certainly to its end
but seeming to be slow and to require patient waiting.

In spite of all the possibilities raised by the superficially simple
language of the introduction to the vision, it is clear that the
prophet and his readers are to expect a direct oracular statement
from the Lord which will answer his complaints, resolve the uncertainties of the moment, and provide a basis for patience during
a period of waiting before the "end."

The Vision (2:4-5)

What follows is a "vision" only in the sense of a prophetic message from God, which could range from the simple "word of the LORD" (I Sam. 3:1) to the graphic visions of Daniel (Dan. 8:1 and following). The vision granted to Habakkuk combines a word of assurance to the faithful and words of warning to the arrogant and greedy. Uncertainties in the text make the precise meaning of the lines of the vision difficult to determine, but the combination of assurance and warning is entirely clear.

The warnings concern him "whose soul is not upright" (2:4a), "the arrogant man," and those—evidently the Chaldeans—whose greed leads them to collect "all nations" (2:5). Perhaps the oppressive Jews of Habakkuk's time are included among the "not upright" and the "arrogant." The reference to the treachery of wine (the Qumran commentary has "wealth" for wine) is not clear, since the parallel line is obscure; both lines appear to refer to the heady effect of overpowering greed demonstrated in the insatiable conquests of the Chaldeans or in the oppressions of Jerusalem's nobility during Jehoiakim's time. Even the warning is not clear, since the word "shall fail" of verse 4a is a conjecture; its actual content is left for the woes of 2:6-19.

The heart of the message of Habakkuk is found in the half verse (2:4b) which directs attention to the righteous. As at 1:4 and 1:13 the word "righteous" must be taken in the relative sense it commonly has in the Old Testament. "The righteous" is the man who "speaks truth from his heart; who does not slander with his tongue . . . and does not take a bribe against the innocent" (Ps. 15:2-5). Habakkuk does not evidence the awareness the Apostle Paul had of the impossibility of achieving a righteousness acceptable to God. The God-fearing oppressed man and the sympathetic prophet of pre-exilic Hebrew times applied this term to themselves as believing men, or men of the Covenant.

Use of Habakkuk's words by the Apostle Paul has somewhat obscured the message of assurance for the believing righteous of the period just before the fall of Jerusalem. Paul's use of the term "faith" as the acceptance of God's gracious work in Christ and as personal commitment to Christ goes far beyond the meaning of Habakkuk's word. With Habakkuk faith means "faithfulness," as the marginal note indicates. When the oracle from God declares that the righteous shall live by his faith, the righteous believer is to understand that the means of his continued life through difficulty and oppression is to be his steadfast effort to maintain his righteousness and to avoid the behavior for which a divinely approved disaster is stored up. His behavior, then, is an effort to avoid the sort of thing indicated in the woes which follow. God did not grant Habakkuk or the oppressed believer of ancient Israel a complete answer to the burdensome question; instead, the ancient believer was asked to continue steadfast in the effort to obey the ethical aspects of divine instruction. The divine oracle promises life through such steadfastness and faith. Such is the answer to the prophet's complaints.

THE FIVE TAUNTS

Habakkuk 2:6-20

The Viewpoint of the "Woes" (2:6a)

At the end of the divine oracle the prophet or an editor introduces the series of five stanzas of threats against those who have prospered in their wickedness. The first half of verse 6 is a question which ascribes the series of woes to the peoples referred to in verse 5, who will one day be in a position to deride their former oppressors. Thus, in the actual setting of the book the series of taunts appears to be the language of oppressed believers rather than of God. Unlike the long taunt poem of Nahum (Nahum 2-3) where the Lord himself speaks (Nahum 2:13 and 3:5-6), the taunts of Habakkuk express only the point of view of a human observer who is a believer in the Lord.

The Taunt Against the Cruel Plunderer (2:6b-8)

The first "woe" is directed against the plunderer, but it concerns two specific areas. The first expression is general, pronouncing a woe to one "who heaps up what is not his own" and continuing with a specific reference to a local oppressor who "loads himself with pledges." Before the end of the stanza, however, attention is redirected to a world power which has "plundered many nations." In the taunts, as in the dialogue with God, this twofold concern appears, on the one hand with oppression within the Judean state and on the other with oppression from a foreign power. The two aspects of oppression can be distinguished some of the time, but in the third and fourth woes they merge into single statements. Any effort to separate an original form of the woes from a reworking of them is doomed to failure.

The Judean oppressor may well be Jehoiakim, whose building operations were condemned by Jeremiah (Jer. 22:13-17), but the foreign oppressor appears to be Assyria rather than Babylon, whose plundering of the nations was just beginning in Jehoiakim's time.

For both the oppressive creditor at home and the plundering world power the woe pronounces a definite doom: retribution. For the one, it is the debtors who will suddenly arise, and for the other, "all the remnant of the peoples shall plunder you." In either case the retribution is a direct result of the ill will produced by the oppression. God is not mentioned, and presumably he only permits the retaliation. The taunt anticipates the human reaction.

The Taunt Against the Greedy Builder (2:9-11)

The second taunt is directed against one who has used evil gain for the building of his house, and again the oppression of Judean by Judean (Jehoiakim?) merges into the oppression of God's people by foreigners (Chaldeans or Assyrians?) who have cut off "many peoples." In either case the house that has been built with evil in an effort to reach earthly security will itself "cry out" against the evildoer. Again the principle of retaliation is strongly stated, though the means of retaliation is expressed through figurative language. Even the "cutting off [of] many peoples" will be matched by a forfeit of life (vs. 10). What is said rests upon a strong sense of justice, but it is not explicitly said that this is the action of God.

The Taunt Against the Guilty City Builder (2:12-14)

The third taunt is directed against one who founds and builds a city with blood-guilt (compare Micah 3:10), that is, after military conquest of an area or after an assassination. No historical allusion can be detected.

Having uttered the word of woe, the prophet-poet indicates his belief that people of the various nations will not forever allow themselves to be used for the vanity ("naught") of their leaders. But it is also the prophet's belief that the attitude found in the peoples is "from the LORD of hosts."

The final declaration of the third taunt is a somewhat modified quotation of Isaiah 11:9. It is an attempt to set forth an attitude opposite to that of the iniquitous builders of cities: for the righteous it remains certain that in the future the earth "will be filled with the knowledge of the glory of the LORD," an all-encompassing blessedness the very opposite of the "fire" and "nothingness" for which the peoples of the nations have been forced to work. It is thus not according to the purpose of God that towns should be built with blood and that the nations should weary themselves to no avail. All such efforts, the reader must understand, will fail; only the glory of the Lord lasts to fill the earth.

The Taunt Against One Who Makes His Neighbors Drunk (2:15-17)

The fourth "woe" concerns one who leads his neighbors into drunkenness and immodesty. Like the first two taunts it sees the fitting punishment in terms of humiliation and disgrace like that he has caused. The text of this taunt is somewhat confused, but the meaning is not obscured by the difficulties which exist. The taunt describes the evildoer as one who enjoys the humiliation of his neighbors when he can make them drunk; "his wrath" is not anger against the neighbors, but ill will, the desire to see them humiliated. Such an attitude may appropriately be ascribed either to an individual in the community or to a nation in relation to other nations.

Retaliation in the form of similar humiliation comes from the Lord's right hand, and instead of glory the evildoer will find shame. "Glory" is to be understood as "reputation"; the oppressor's reputation may have been good, but divine justice will bring shame and disgrace in its place. This is the thought of Nahum (3:5-7) with regard to the reputation of Nineveh.

Thus far (2:15-16) the fourth woe has expressed only figuratively the shame and disgrace threatened for an oppressing nation. In verse 17 the figurative expression of drunkenness and shame gives way to a reference to "the violence done to Lebanon" by the various invading nations. The oppressing nation against which the taunts are directed—whether Assyria or Babylon—will reap what it has sowed: bloodshed and violence both to the land and to the cities. The principle of appropriate judgment, where the punishment fits the crime, is applicable both to individuals and to nations.

The Taunt Against the Makers of Idols (2:18-20)

The final taunt does not begin with the word "woe" as do the others, but with a question regarding the value of an idol to its maker. The absurdity of idolatry is clearly stated in the poet's next declaration, "For the workman trusts in his own creation when he makes dumb idols!" Finally the "woe" is expressed against anyone who calls for a word of revelation from "a wooden thing." Visualizing the construction of the idol, the prophet sees that "there is no breath at all in it," and hence it cannot offer any significant word.

In contrast "the LORD is in his holy temple," and all of the earth may profitably keep silence before him, not primarily in awe-struck worship but to hear and receive instruction, as in Micah 4:1-4 and Isaiah 2:2-4. The similarity in thought to Isaiah 44:9-11, which is generally considered to date from after the fall of Jerusalem, and the lack of relationship to the other taunts of the chapter, have suggested to many that the fifth stanza as a whole is an addition by an exilic or postexilic scribe or editor. On the other hand, it is not safe to be dogmatic, for Habakkuk has already referred to the false worship of the oppressing nation (1:11 and 16), and it is not impossible that he sensed and expressed the futility of idolatry some sixty years before the Prophet of the Exile developed the theme. It was, in fact, the conception of God as the living God which led Habakkuk to his problem. The concern of God for the purity of his people could not exclude concern for the purity of the instruments he would use in chastising his people, for God is a personal Being. Because God is personal, he may be addressed with such complaints as Habakkuk has uttered for his people, and he responds with such oracles as have been included in the book. Because God is personal, the law of just punishment for evils committed operates in the created world. The series of taunts voiced for the peoples of the world by the prophet indicates confidence in the operation of this law. No idol can respond in this personal way, even though it may be addressed as a personal being by an idolater. But the Lord can and will speak from his holy temple.

THE PSALM OF HABAKKUK

Habakkuk 3:1-19

Title (3:1)

The third section of the Book of Habakkuk begins with a new title (3:1), as though the third chapter were an appendix. It is interesting but not necessarily significant that the commentary on Habakkuk found at Qumran is concerned quite clearly with only the first two chapters of the book. Since other commentaries found at Qumran are also concerned with sections of books or with individual psalms, this fact by itself does not prove anything regarding the length of the contents of the book as it was extant among the people of Qumran.

The psalm is definitely ascribed to Habakkuk "the prophet" and is described as a "prayer." In spite of arguments to the contrary, it is appropriate for Habakkuk. The psalm is a prayer for the renewal of God's ancient work. The vision reviewing God's activity touches events of the earliest periods of Hebrew history, and the final expressions of confidence and joy in the Lord are an appropriate response to the oracle of 2:4b.

The meaning of the expression "according to Shigionoth" (compare the title of Ps. 7) has been the subject of much discussion and remains in doubt: some have been led by the Greek version and by the note at the end of the psalm to make a slight change so as to translate it "on the stringed instruments"; others prefer to derive the sense of "a lamentation" from an Akkadian word with the same root. The meaning of the word "Selah" found at verses 3, 9, and 13 is also undetermined, but its appearance probably indicates liturgical use of the prayer.

The Opening Petition (3:2)

The prayer opens with an address to the Lord, which declares the poet's fear of the action of the Lord and asks for a renewal of his work "in the midst of the years." Much is expressed in the brevity of this verse: the poet has been told of the work of the Lord; he feels a sense of awe as he recollects what God has done; in his time no clear evidence of divine activity has been known; his time may thus be considered as a time of "wrath" in contrast to the earlier time of "mercy." "Mercy" refers to the gracious

activity of God on behalf of his people which is about to be described, while "wrath" suggests the absence of such gracious work
and hence a sense of being under divine displeasure.

When God Came from Teman (3:3-15)

The heart of the prayer is an extended description of the coming of God from Mount Paran in Teman, set forth in highly
graphic figures of speech with brief historical allusions.

Though God is addressed as the "LORD" at one point in this
section (vs. 8, where some commentators believe the word should
be omitted), the vision begins with the unusual word for God
(Eloah) found throughout most of the Book of Job and elsewhere in scattered instances throughout the exilic and postexilic
literature. Although used in what appear to be late sources and
often in connection with foreign settings, this word for God is often
associated with ideas of creation and redemption. Particularly in
Deuteronomy 32:15, 18; Proverbs 30:5; Psalms 18:32; 50:22;
114:7; and Nehemiah 9:17, as in the psalm of Habakkuk, this
word is related to the familiar Exodus narrative which is described in terms of the appearance of God through a violent
storm. Many of the elements of Habakkuk's prayer may also be
found in the other passages in which this name for God appears.

The reference to Teman and Mount Paran points to the area
of desert inhabited in historic times by the Edomites, east of the
Arabah, that dry valley extending south from the Dead Sea to the
Gulf of Aqabah, and to the area south of Kadesh-barnea and
west of the Arabah. To this desolate and terrifying area, to which
also Cushan and Midian in verse 7 refer, the Hebrew people
looked back in connection with the experiences which followed the
Exodus. From here God had manifested his power. In the figurative (but difficult) language of one form of the familiar tradition,
the prayer of Habakkuk recalls this revelation of God's power.

God is visualized as possessing a surpassing brightness as he
comes from the dazzling desert area of Teman. His march toward
the settled lands is accompanied by "pestilence" and "plague";
these should probably be printed with capital letters as names of
demons (actually once the deities of Semitic tribes). As the vision
proceeds, the poet watches while God stands and measures the
earth, looks at and shakes the nations, and scatters "the eternal
mountains." Cushan and Midian in particular tremble from his
nearness and power.

Naturally the heat and brightness of God's presence affect the rivers (vss. 8-10), drying up those of the desert and cleaving the mountainous regions with new streams of raging waters. So also the mountains and the deep are affected, the one writhing and the other giving forth its roar as the manifestation of God takes the form of a thunderstorm. The lightning of the storm is pictured as arrows (vss. 9, 11), familiar in representations of deity from ancient Greece as well as from the eastern world; sun and moon are temporarily hidden, seeming to stand still for the duration of the storm.

The Lord, the Holy God, is now addressed directly in words depicting his action through the theophany: bestriding the earth in furious anger, he tramples the nations; going forth for the salvation of his people, he crushes and pierces the head of the wicked. The final verse (15) of the poetic recollection of God's appearance seems to identify the terrible events of the storm with the destruction of the Egyptians at the Red Sea at the beginning of the Exodus, but it must be admitted that if this identification had not been made elsewhere (as, for example, in Psalm 77), it would not be clear at this point.

Meditation and Response to the Appearance of God (3:16-19)

The remaining verses of the psalm express the poet's reflection upon the ancient theophany which he has just recalled, and then in noble language he asserts his own joyful dependence upon the God of his salvation.

His first reaction to the recollected vision is a feeling of help-lessness and terror (vs. 16), but quickly his spirit is calmed as he determines to wait quietly for the day of trouble to come upon the invaders of his time.

Then he returns to the thought of God who is a "present help in trouble." Though the economy of his land be ruined by the devastations of the enemy, Habakkuk can conclude, "Yet I will rejoice in the LORD, I will joy in the God of my salvation." The real and vital presence of God gives him strength and a sense of triumph which goes beyond the patience and perseverance called for by the declaration, "The righteous shall live by his faith." To the noble expression of faith in the concluding verses of this psalm many persecuted saints have returned through the centuries. Does it not deserve to be used again?

THE BOOK OF

ZEPHANIAH

INTRODUCTION

The Prophet and His Times

Zephaniah is the first identifiable prophet to bring the word of the Lord to Judah after Isaiah's latest utterances in connection with the siege of Jerusalem by Sennacherib in 701 B.C. During the reign of King Manasseh (687-642 B.C.) the only reported word from God is a judgment on that reign, which "the LORD said by his servants the prophets" (II Kings 21:10). No other prophetic word is reported during the reigns of Manasseh and Amon (642-640 B.C.).

According to the title of the Book of Zephaniah the word of the Lord came to this prophet "in the days of Josiah the son of Amon," which indicates a possible date from 640 B.C. to 609 B.C. The title also indicates the ancestry of the prophet back to the fourth generation, to a person named Hezekiah. Whether Zephaniah's ancestor was the Hezekiah who was king of Judah in Isaiah's time cannot be determined. The editor of the book does not indicate that the Hezekiah mentioned was the king, but nowhere else is a prophet's ancestry listed back for four generations.

Looking back from the period of Josiah's reign, a Judean could reflect on the unwholesome reign of King Manasseh, many of the evils of which no doubt persisted in Josiah's reign. He could also reflect on the extent to which Assyrian influence had affected Judean life, particularly with relation to the introduction of the worship of sun, moon, and stars, referred to in II Kings 21:3, and the introduction of foreign clothing, referred to in Zephaniah 1:8. A prophet of the period would no doubt have been aware of a growing weakness on the Assyrian throne after the death of Ashurbanipal (about 633 B.C.), and he may well have sensed that the end of the Assyrian Empire was approaching.

Coincident with the weakness of the Assyrian throne, stirrings of revolt and of independence developed rapidly in the two ends of the Near Eastern world: under the energetic Twenty-sixth Dynasty Egypt became free of Assyrian control and in the latter part of Josiah's reign began to push into Syria; in the east the Medes, under the leadership of Cyaxares, made an unsuccessful attack on Nineveh about 625 B.C., and about the same time Babylon declared its independence from Assyria.

Another power was on the horizon during the last half of the seventh century before Christ. To what extent Zephaniah was concerned with the nomadic Scythians has been debated without a clear conclusion. It is known that the Scythians first reached the northern borders of Assyria during the latter part of the eighth century, and that they continued to exert pressure alternately upon Assyria and Media and later upon Persia. In 612 B.C. they joined with the Medes and Babylonians in the final attack upon Nineveh. Herodotus, the historian, reports what appears to have been an earlier nomadic raid against Egypt and the destruction of a temple at the Philistine town of Ashkelon during the reign of Psammeticus (I or II?) of Egypt. Although the date of this raid is uncertain, some students have believed that it is reflected in the earliest prophecies of Jeremiah and in the prophecy of Zephaniah. Actually, neither prophet names the Scythians, and many recent students do not see any evidence of the Scythians in either Jeremiah or Zephaniah. Certainly the evidence is not clear enough to date Zephaniah's work by the Scythian raid.

The work of Zephaniah cannot be dated any more accurately by referring to his messages directed against the foreign nations (Zeph. 2:4-15). The reference to Nineveh (2:13-15) suggests that the prophecy preceded the fall of that city in 612 B.C., and the reference to the Philistine cities (2:4-7) has often been used in connection with Herodotus' brief word concerning a Scythian raid to the borders of Egypt to indicate the period around 625 B.C. All of the references to foreign nations in the second chapter, however, look forward to complete destruction of the peoples involved, and therefore cannot be linked with any particular attacks or invasions even if these were clearly identifiable.

Josiah's reign over Judah is remembered in the Old Testament for his religious reforms (described in II Kings 22-23), including the renovation of the Temple and his efforts to purify the worship of God in and around Jerusalem. Insofar as he deals with Judah, Zephaniah (1:2-18) is concerned with some of the same evils as Josiah, though his language is not limited to the religious abuses referred to in II Kings (see the comment on Zeph. 1:7-9).

Though it is clear that Zephaniah was concerned with abuses which Josiah tried to end, apparently he did not preach in direct support of the reform movement. Rather, he seems either to have preached a few years prior to the reforms of 621 B.C. or during the time of Jehoiakim, when many of the abuses seem to have been resumed (compare Jer. 32:29-35). Thus Zephaniah's work was probably carried on during the period just prior to the reforms of Josiah, about 625 B.C., but it is not impossible that he labored in Jehoiakim's time (609-598 B.C.) and was wrongly assigned by an editor to Josiah's reign.

The Message of Zephaniah

Zephaniah's message is very largely concerned with "the day of the LORD," which he sees as a day of the destructive outpouring of God's wrath upon all men, involving particularly the evildoers of Judah and Jerusalem, but also the proud and boastful foreign nations which oppressed Judah at various times.

The expression "the day of the LORD" perhaps originated in a battle cry as a part of the general conception of the holy war waged by the early Israelites, and as such it probably includes elements of the ancient story of the victory of God over the chaos at the time of the creation. As a day of victory it was associated before the time of Amos with expectations of peace and prosperity, but after his preaching (Amos 5:18-20) it came to have threatening aspects for Israel and Judah. In any case the Day of the Lord always refers to the time when his will is accomplished, and this will includes the destruction of the workers of evil.

In Zephaniah "the day of the LORD" recalls the setting of battle, with the destruction of life and property which belongs to military conflict, and promises distress and terror as well as the destruction of battle for the people of Judah, for the foreign nations mentioned, and for all flesh. Zephaniah does not emphasize the earthquakes and other physical phenomena sometimes connected with the Day of the Lord (Joel 2:10-11). On the Day of the Lord, as Zephaniah sees it, evildoers will be cut off from their positions of power and luxury and their cities will be destroyed. Only a few expressions may be considered to refer to the outpouring of God's wrath on the realm of nature, as, for example, Zephaniah 1:2-3.

With Zephaniah the reason for the wrath of God is clear,

whether its application is toward Judah or toward foreign nations. In either case the fundamental fault is false worship—the worship of false gods and the rebellious refusal to seek the Lord. Zephaniah's message is not primarily directed toward the relationships between men as the messages of Amos and of Micah are. Instead he is concerned because men have acted in pride rather than in humility; they have boastfully oppressed their neighboring states or have sat thickening upon their lees, thinking, "The LORD will not do good, nor will he do ill" (Zeph. 1:12). Against such practical irreligion is heard the word of God through Zephaniah, "I will overthrow the wicked" (1:3). Such a word from God is relevant in every age when men do not find a warning in the destruction of cities and do not "accept correction" from God.

The book, however, presents a hopeful aspect, whether it is the work of Zephaniah himself or of an editor. In the last chapter the book turns from threats to promises and invites the humble and lowly to look forward to a day of victory and restoration after the day of wrath. Thus the true mission of the prophet is preserved: to warn of impending evil and to urge people to turn from evil ways, and to offer prospect of blessing if they respond to the call of God.

OUTLINE

Title. Zephaniah 1:1

The Day of the Lord. Zephaniah 1:2—3:20

Concerning Judah and Jerusalem (1:2-13)
The Great Day of the Wrath of the Lord (1:14—2:3)
Concerning Foreign Nations (2:4-15)
The Indignation of the Lord (3:1-8)
The Victory of the Lord (3:9-20)

COMMENTARY

TITLE

Zephaniah 1:1

In common with most of the prophetic books, Zephaniah begins with a title which defines the prophet's ancestry and the time
of his ministry and which also characterizes his work. Since we
cannot be certain that the Hezekiah mentioned was the Judean
king of the end of the eighth century before Christ, the genealogical
data are tantalizing rather than helpful. The question of the date
of the prophet's work has been discussed above (see Introduction). The book is characterized simply as "the word of the
LORD," indicating probably an oral delivery of the principal messages during the time of Josiah.

THE DAY OF THE LORD

Zephaniah 1:2—3:20

Concerning Judah and Jerusalem (1:2-13)

The Sweeping of the Lord (1:2-6)

The initial section of Zephaniah's prophecy does not use the
expression "day of the LORD" or any other expressions often associated with it, such as "that day." Nevertheless, its content clearly
unites it with the rest of the chapter in which the prophet refers
specifically to his central theme. In a vigorous series of declarations the Lord himself announces his plans with regard to a
"cleaning up" operation which will affect the whole earth and
particularly Judah and Jerusalem.

The operation is described as a sweeping away of everything—
man, beast, birds, and fish (which were not destroyed by the
Flood). All nature is affected, though God's particular concern
is "the wicked," or "the stumbling blocks" as the word appears in
the Hebrew. The human race will be cut off by the action of the
Lord.

Turning directly to Judah and Jerusalem, the Lord threatens to cut off "from this place the remnant of Baal and the name of the idolatrous priests" (1:4), together with three groups of false worshipers among the inhabitants of Jerusalem.

Canaanite Baal worship was evidently practiced in and around Jerusalem during the time of Manasseh and Amon (II Kings 21:3 and 21) and was not finally eradicated by the reforms of Josiah (see Jer. 32:29). "Idolatrous priests" in the Old Testament always minister to foreign gods or offer worship unacceptable to the Lord (compare II Kings 23:5). Worship of the sun, moon, and stars from the tops of the roofs of various buildings as late as the time of Zedekiah is attested by Jeremiah (Jer. 19:13 and 32:29). The high place near Jerusalem dedicated to the Ammonite deity, Milcom, was destroyed by Josiah (II Kings 23:13) along with high places dedicated to other gods of neighboring peoples, but it is likely that Jehoiakim permitted the worship of these deities to be re-established (II Kings 23:37).

The determination of the Lord to sweep everything away from the face of the earth meant the cutting off of false worship from Judah and Jerusalem in particular. Thus the simple, blunt message of Zephaniah begins.

The Lord's Sacrificial Feast (1:7-9)

In a second poetic oracle, still expressing the word of the Lord himself, there comes a call to a sacrificial meal in which the language of the ancient ritual receives a telling new content.

The stanza begins with a single word—similar to the English word "Hush!"—perhaps used in quieting the noise of worshipers before the beginning of a ritual. (See its use in Habakkuk 2:20 and Zechariah 2:13, where prophetically the Gentile world is called to silence before the Lord.) The prophet announces that the moment for the ritual is at hand, here described as "the day of the LORD." In keeping with the archaic character of Zephaniah's figurative language, the expression "the day of the LORD" has here the sense of expected good for God's Chosen People, a sense which Amos repudiated (5:18-20).

Graciously the Lord has prepared his sacrifice and consecrated his guests, as Samuel prepared for a sacrifice in Bethlehem before anointing young David to be king (I Sam. 16:2-5). Such an occasion was perhaps not infrequently a time when guests were recognized, as David was honored and as Saul had been honored with a special portion earlier (I Sam. 9:22-24).

But abruptly, after again mentioning "the LORD's sacrifice," the prophet introduces a jarring note: the Lord himself announces punishment upon the guests, arrayed as they are in fine—but foreign— attire. The punishment will fall upon officials and the king's sons, and upon "every one who leaps over the threshold, and those who fill their master's house with violence and fraud." The leaping over the threshold may refer to a superstitious ritual of stepping across the threshold of a temple, such as that described in I Samuel 5:5 in connection with the priests of the Philistine god Dagon, or it may be a ritual of worship on a podium upon which an idol was placed. In either case, the act represents the performance of a pagan or superstitious ritual indicating a lack of genuine faith in God. With the terms "violence and fraud" Zephaniah turns from the area of ritual to the more familiar ethical ground of the prophets.

"That Day" in Jerusalem (1:10-13)

The next stanza of the prophet's message is a descriptive passage, in which the sounds and sights of a day of catastrophe are successively given brief attention. Between the sounds and the sights are two words from the Lord, addressed to the people of the city.

The sounds are cries from various parts of the city: the "Fish Gate" (also mentioned in Neh. 3:3; 12:39) was apparently at a point on the northern edge of the city; the "Second Quarter" is identified only as the area in which the prophetess Huldah had her dwelling (II Kings 22:14), perhaps in the recently developed section of the city enclosed by Manasseh (II Chron. 33:14). Should "the hills" be considered another sectional name, or were they simply the hills upon which the city was built? The "Mortar" may be the Tyropoeon Valley in the middle of Jerusalem, perhaps used as a market place in the time of Zephaniah. God's address is particularly to the inhabitants of the Mortar, where trade will apparently be interrupted when invasion from the north arrives.

God himself promises to "search Jerusalem with lamps"—like Diogenes—and to punish the men who have thought to themselves, "The LORD will not do good, nor will he do ill." Such men are like wine that has been left to stand too long and which has become thickened with sediment. Their accumulations of houses and vineyards will be laid waste. "That day" will be a day of devastation and disruption of the ordinary business of the city.

The Great Day of the Wrath of the Lord (1:14—2:3)

The Distressing End of Humanity (1:14-18)

The remaining section of chapter 1 surveys the "day of the LORD" more broadly, characterizing it in several descriptive phrases and declaring the Lord's determination to bring a distressing end upon the inhabitants of the earth. In this passage "the day of the LORD" reverts to the world-wide concerns of 1:2-3 as distinguished from the specific concern with Judah and Jerusalem displayed in 1:4-13.

The prophet first declares that the Day of the Lord is near and hastening fast, emphasizing the suddenness with which destruction could come and the imminence of the divine intervention in human affairs.

A series of descriptive phrases characterizes the bitterness, distress, and devastation of the day, noting the shouts of anguish of the mighty man, the clouds and darkness (of smoke from burning buildings or of volcanic eruption?), and the trumpet blasts which strike terror to the hearts of all participants in battle. It is through the purpose of God that such distress comes to men. They walk without direction like the blind, because they have sinned against the Lord.

In the conflict blood is poured out; flesh is exposed and left to rot upon the ground; the earth will be consumed in the fire of God's wrath, and no possessions of silver or gold will provide deliverance. The inhabitants of the earth will come to a "full, yea, sudden end."

Above all else it must be noted that the day of wrath, distress, destruction, and death is the Lord's day. It is his doing; his anger has been aroused because of sin committed against himself. The false worship, violence, and fraud of Jerusalem and Judah have provided illustrations of the sins responsible for God's wrath against his people; sins of other nations will be mentioned in chapter 2. In Paul's words, "all have sinned" (Rom. 3:23), and hence all will be punished. To Zephaniah the end of the whole human race appears imminent.

Calls to the Shameless and to the Humble (2:1-3)

Zephaniah issues a summons to the "shameless nation" and an invitation to the humble of the land. Though the references to

Philistine cities in verse 4 are attached to this stanza in the Revised Standard Version, there is no reason to identify the "shameless nation" with Philistia, and in view of the invitation to the humble in verse 3 there is more reason to think that the first three verses of the chapter offer Judah a last opportunity.

The shameless nation is called to assemble in one last effort to avert the fierce anger of the Lord. The first clause of verse 2 is somewhat obscure because of textual difficulties, but it seems to suggest the possibility that a chance remains of turning aside the swiftly moving and imminent destruction described in 1:14-18. At least the humble of the land may be hidden on the day of wrath, if they seek righteousness and humility and do God's commands.

Concerning Foreign Nations (2:4-15)

Philistia (2:4-7)

The prophet's declarations regarding the foreign nations begin with a statement concerning the Philistine land and cities. Using a rich variety of terms to designate the coastal area inhabited by the Philistines, Zephaniah announces complete destruction and desolation, and then looks beyond the destruction to see its reassignment as the possession of Judah.

Four of the five cities which once made up the Philistine league (see Joshua 13:3) are mentioned here by name, and for each an aspect of the coming destruction is specified. The prophet then pronounces a "woe" upon the Philistines as "inhabitants of the seacoast" and as "nation of the Cherethites," an expression parallel to "Philistines" in Ezekiel 25:16 and possibly indicating the Cretan origin of the Philistines. The prophet uses the word "Canaan" for the land inhabited by the Philistines to designate what remained of Canaanite culture in Zephaniah's time.

So thoroughly will the area be destroyed that the coastal region will be used only for a pasture land, but then the remnant of the house of Judah will lead flocks into it and allow them to lie down "in the houses of Ashkelon [a Philistine city] . . . at evening."

Because no clear historical allusion can be identified in this word against Philistia, a setting for these verses is difficult to determine. Verse 7, with its references to Judah and the restoration of fortune (or possibly the "return from exile"), may be exilic or postexilic. The remainder of the threat makes no clear reference to the Egyptian siege of Ashdod or the Scythian destruction of the temple of Ashkelon reported by Herodotus. Apparently the threat against the Philistines looks beyond any contemporary events to a time when the Lord will make a "full end" of all the inhabitants of the earth—including the Philistines.

But after the "full end" threatened in 1:18, the prophet (or his editors) could see first the possibility that the humble righteous would be hidden in the day of wrath (2:3) and then the assurance that a remnant of the house of Judah would one day be restored to a peaceful nomadic life in the area formerly held by the Philistines.

Actually, in spite of destructions, the Philistine cities continued into New Testament times (Ashdod is known as Azotus in Acts 8:40, and Gaza is mentioned in Acts 8:26), and no complete destruction occurred during Old Testament times.

Moab and Ammon (2:8-11)

In the next part of the section concerning foreign nations the Lord notes that the Moabites and the Ammonites (here linked together because both peoples were on Judah's eastern flank) have made boasts against his people and their territory. In the language of an oath, God announces coming destruction for them. Moab and Ammon will become like Sodom and Gomorrah, "a land possessed by nettles and salt pits, and a waste for ever."

But again the prophet (or his editors) took a second look and saw the remnant of God's people possessing—even plundering—these peoples who had "scoffed and boasted against the people of the LORD of hosts."

Before turning to another nation the prophet makes a general statement concerning all the lands of the nations and their various gods. "The LORD will be terrible against them," says Zephaniah; "yea, he will famish all the gods of the earth, and to him shall bow down, each in its place, all the lands of the nations." God is completely superior to any other gods and to the peoples who worship them. In view of the boasts made against the territory— and hence in effect against the person—of God, the Lord makes his threat with the oath "as I live." In earlier days the oath "as the Lord lives" was common on the lips of Israelites, but among the later prophets (particularly in Ezekiel) the words of God himself are supported by the oath in the form found in Zephaniah. The oath points to the living nature of the affronted Lord, and suggests the certainty of his retribution against those who have uttered boasts against him.

Ethiopia (2:12)

Zephaniah addresses the Ethiopians and deals with them in a single verse. The term "Ethiopians" (normally the people south of the first cataract of the Nile) probably stands for all Egypt, which was ruled by an Ethiopian dynasty for a period ending at about 650 B.C. These people—whether Egypt and Ethiopia taken together or Ethiopia alone—"shall be slain by my sword."

Assyria (2:13-15)

The final message against a foreign nation concerns Assyria and her capital, Nineveh. The prophet declares that the Lord will stretch his hand toward the north and will destroy Nineveh and its surrounding area, making it a "lair for wild beasts." Though the prophet mentions "herds" (vs. 14) as lying in the midst of the once inhabited city, he emphasizes rather that the fate of Nineveh is to be a place for a variety of wild animals or birds, whose identities are obscured because of uncertainties in the Hebrew text (see margin).

Speaking for the passer-by, the prophet looks contemptuously at the ruins of the city and reflects how Nineveh had "dwelt secure" and said to herself, "I am and there is none else." The statement of Nineveh (identical with that of Babylon in Isaiah 47:8, 10) is roughly parallel to God's "I am the LORD, and there is no other" (Isa. 45:5, 6, 18, 21). The exilic prophet exposes the full blasphemy of the boastings of Nineveh and Babylon, but Zephaniah was sensitive enough to quote them and to allow his readers or hearers to draw their own conclusions. Such self-sufficient security is always blasphemous, and even in the twentieth century A.D. it invites God's action in order to bring about a proper sense of humility.

The Indignation of the Lord (3:1-8)

The final chapter of the Book of Zephaniah is a mixture of elements of varied character, the first ones threatening but the later ones sounding a strong cry of encouragement. Verses 1-2 appear to be transitional, continuing the spirit of the prophecies against the foreign nations but bringing the direct application of God's indignation back to Jerusalem. Although the rebellious, defiled, and oppressing city is not named in the section which refers to it (3:1-7), it is clear from the pronouns and from the references to the Lord and to the Law that it is Jerusalem.

Woe to the Rebellious City (3:1-2)

The prophet's first declaration is a word of "woe" upon this city, together with a fourfold explanation of the threat: Jerusalem has not accepted correction; she has not listened to the voice of God as communicated through the prophets; she does not trust God; she does not draw near to him in penitent worship. Because of this recalcitrance she may expect disaster on the Day of the Lord.

Wicked Leaders and Righteous God (3:3-5)

The next section of the statement regarding Jerusalem specifies four groups of leaders and characterizes their sins, using the imagery of wild animals and also more conventional religious language. Ezekiel 22:25-28 and Micah 3 provide parallels to this passage, enlarging on the details. The "officials" are members of the nobility; the "judges" represent members of the ruling class, the elders of good family who met regularly in the gate of the city to settle disputes. Instead of being shepherds (as the ideal ruler appears in Micah 5:4 and in Zech. 11:4), these rulers are like the wild animals that immediately tear and devour whatever prey falls their way. But priests and prophets are no better; they are men without character who do not preserve the distinction between holy and profane and who provide instruction which does violence to the true guidance of God found in the Law.

Only the Lord does no wrong within the rebellious city; he remains constant and is always righteous. Evidence of his justice is to be seen daily at the return of the dawn. Men continue to yield to the temptations that come with power and positions of leadership, and soon lose any sense of shame in the evil they do; only God is always righteous.

The Unlearned Lesson (3:6-7)

The prophet speaks for the Lord, pointing to the destruction which has been wrought on other nations, and calling attention to the lesson such destruction should have brought to Jerusalem. Nations have been "cut off"; they are desolate and in ruins follow-

ing the destruction of war. But the lesson which Jerusalem and
Judah might have learned through such devastation has been lost.
Her people or her leaders ("they" is indefinite) eagerly make
their deeds yet more corrupt.

The Decisive Day of Wrath (3:8)

Thus far in the third chapter the prophet (or his editor) has
centered attention on the rebellion of Jerusalem, on the character
of its leaders, and on the refusal to learn the lesson of the conquered cities of neighboring nations. In all of this there has been
no reference to the central theme of the book, the Day of the
Lord. Now, in a transitional verse, we hear the voice of the Lord
promising his decisive day of the gathering of the nations for the
outpouring of his wrath.

The outpouring of wrath threatens the destruction of all the
earth, for the Lord has decided to gather the various nations to
hear his "witness." Whereas in Micah 6, God calls upon the hills
and mountains to listen to his testimony against his people, here
the witness is against all the assembled nations of the world. No
one can escape the heat of his anger. Zephaniah, like his contemporaries, Jeremiah and Habakkuk, is concerned with the evil in
all men, not just with the evil of the people of God.

In what spirit is the command to "wait" uttered? Addressed
to a plural subject, it is not an invitation to the prophet to see
God carry out his plans upon all peoples. It is rather an invitation
to any believers who will hear to await quietly the destructive action of God in the hope of survival and blessing (compare 2:3, 7).
The prophets seldom expressed the threats of God without permitting the pious listener to sense some indication of hope.

The Victory of the Lord (3:9-20)

How much the last sections of some of the prophetic books
(notably Isaiah, Micah, and Amos) represent editorial additions
to modify the severely condemnatory tone of the early prophets
cannot be determined with any certainty, but it seems clear that
some sections were added to some of the books by the successors
of the prophets. Many of the additions appear to be efforts to
make the language of the prophets apply more exactly to new conditions in the life of the people, and to show that God's concern
for his people did not come to an end in the Exile but continues

into the new situations that arise in it and beyond it. Such seems to be the case with the Book of Zephaniah, although it is impossible to identify the precise point at which additions began to be made.

The final section of Zephaniah again refers to "that day," but now it is a day in which the victory of the Lord and the restoration of his humble people will be accomplished, instead of a day of wrath for all nations. So men have always found the vision of the victory of the Lord arising phoenixlike out of the ashes of their false hopes and their proud and rebellious boastings.

Gentile Conversion and Jewish Return (3:9-10)

Speaking in the first person, for God, and using an expression parallel to the familiar "on that day," the prophet (or his editor) announces two important developments, which presumably will follow the outpouring of the wrath of God. The one concerns the Gentile peoples who have not served the Lord, while the other affects the scattered Jews of the postexilic age.

The Lord declares that he will change the speech of the peoples to a pure speech, so that they may all call on the name of the Lord and offer united worship. The need for a pure speech arises not from a lack of acquaintance with Hebrew vocabulary, but from impure lips, such as Isaiah was conscious of in his inaugural vision (Isa. 6:5). One step toward the conversion of the nations is provision for the proper language with which to worship God (compare Isa. 19:18 where it is said, "In that day there will be five cities in . . . Egypt which speak the language of Canaan and swear allegiance to the LORD of hosts"). In contrast, on the Day of Pentecost the Apostles were enabled to speak to a mixed crowd so that "each one heard them speaking in his own language" (Acts 2:6).

Scattered Jews, described as "suppliants, the daughter of my dispersed ones" (if this is the proper reading of an uncertain Hebrew text), will bring God's offering from such far-off regions as the land "beyond the rivers of Ethiopia."

Comfort and Purification of Jerusalem (3:11-13)

The next section is clearly addressed to the city of Jerusalem, but it concerns the humble and lowly who will be gathered to her and there find refuge. Again it is God himself who speaks, promising the removal of the haughty from his holy mountain and the shepherding of the Remnant. The city will no more be put to shame, since in that coming day no wrong will be done in it and no lies or deceit uttered. The rebellious deeds of the past will be forgotten (on what basis is not specified), but because of the purification of those who will be left "in Israel" and because of God's promise to provide a refuge, "none shall make them afraid."

God's Victory: the Restoring of Fortune (3:14-20)

The final section of the book continues the address to Zion from God himself and stresses the victory of the Lord without emphasizing the exaltation of his people over other nations as some of the other prophetic writings do (notably Zech. 12-14).

Addressing the people of Jerusalem as "daughter of Zion" and as "Israel," as the reconstituted people of God, God calls for singing and rejoicing (see Zech. 9:9; Isa. 54:1). The reason for joy is similar to what is expressed in the passages from Zechariah and Isaiah, but it is declared in different language: The Lord has eliminated both the enemies who have afflicted his people and the reason for the presence of these enemies—the judgments against her. Instead the Lord himself stands as King in the midst of Jerusalem.

With God in her midst, Jerusalem no longer needs to fear or to be afflicted with weak hands, a condition often figurative but always associated with fearfulness. Instead God is "a warrior who gives victory" (vs. 17) and promises to remove disaster. He will deal with all oppressors and will save the lame and gather the outcast (vs. 19).

Finally, God promises to make his people "renowned and praised among all the peoples of the earth" (vs. 20). Such a promise is far from the bloodthirsty vengeance anticipated in Zechariah 12-14; instead, it is much more in the spirit of the vision of the exaltation of Jerusalem in Micah 4:1-4 and Isaiah 2:2-4. Here in Zephaniah it is consciously combined with a promise to gather the Jews of the dispersion into their home and to restore their fortunes.

Thus, after a full application of the theme of judgment on "the day of the LORD" to Judah and Jerusalem and to some foreign nations, the Book of Zephaniah turns to look beyond the day of wrath and destruction to a time of singing and victory when God will restore the fortunes of his people.

THE BOOK OF

HAGGAI

INTRODUCTION

The Prophet

Almost nothing is known about the prophet Haggai. His name can be translated "festal" and may be an abbreviation of some such name as "Haggiyah," which would mean "festival of the Lord." An ancient tradition suggests that Haggai was of priestly lineage, but there is nothing in the biblical references to confirm or deny this. His concern for the rebuilding of the Temple may have been only that of a layman inspired by the divine call. The records concerning Haggai give no certain information about whether he was among those who had seen the former glory of the house of God, but his concern for the rebuilding of the Temple suggests that he may have witnessed its destruction by the Chaldeans in 587 B.C. Since the prophecies of Haggai are limited to a brief period during the second year of Darius I, it has been guessed that the prophet was an old man and that he did not live to see the dedication of the rebuilt Temple some four years later.

The Composition of the Book

As is the case with the personal history of Haggai, so there is no certainty about the composition of the book. The prophetic words are concerned with God, the Temple, the "times," and the people addressed, never with the prophet. "I" in the book is the Lord, never the prophet. Without the brief introductory narrative portions, even the name of the prophet would be unknown. Two alternative methods of composition may be conjectured: (1) that the prophet himself prepared the entire book, writing in the third person and thus minimizing himself, or (2) that someone else, acquainted with the important work of the prophet, shortly after his ministry set down what he remembered of the prophet's messages, together with the setting in which each was uttered. The second suggestion is preferable, since it is the more natural explanation of the third person narrative. The sketchy nature of the narrative passages suggests that the book was actually recorded very soon after the events took place, possibly at the actual dedication of the rebuilt Temple (in 516 B.C.; see Ezra 6:14-15), when recollections of the beginning of the project would appropriately be brought to mind.

Haggai's Ministry

The purpose of Haggai's ministry was clearly to stir his contemporaries to honor God through the rebuilding of the Temple. His words all bear on this subject and are concerned with other subjects—such as the hard times and the shaking of the nations —only as they are related to the reconstruction of the Temple.

The book's purpose is to preserve the words of Haggai for others beyond his immediate contemporaries. But this purpose is not merely to honor the man or men responsible for the rebuilding of the Temple or to recount the progress of the project. The permanent message of the book is to be found in the interrelationship between the words of God and the conditions and responses of the people addressed, and may perhaps best be summed up in the briefest single utterance of God through the prophet, "I am with you, says the LORD" (1:13). It is for this assurance that the book has been preserved and included in the canon of the Old Testament. In the midst of the difficult times of an earlier day God spoke to his people and stirred them to honor him and thus to find blessing; at all times he is able and willing to be with his people and even to shake the nations on their behalf.

The Book of Haggai consists of a brief series of words "of the LORD" which came by Haggai the prophet to the returned exiles during the second year of Darius I, king of Persia. These words are set in a sketchy narrative which provides the reader with the month and day of each utterance and with an identification of the recipients of the divine message.

OUTLINE

COMMENTARY

THE HARD TIMES IN THE SECOND YEAR OF DARIUS

Haggai 1:1-11

The Setting (1:1)

The Book of Haggai begins by defining the setting of the prophet's work. The first word of the Lord came to Haggai in the year 520 B.C., two years after Darius Hystaspes had killed the usurper Gaumata (or Gomates) and had thus regained control of the Persian Empire for the Achaemenid Dynasty. The first message came "in the sixth month, on the first day of the month," approximately the first of September. It was delivered by the prophet to the two principal personages of Jerusalem. These were the Persian-approved governor of the Judean subdivision of the satrapy "beyond the River" (that is, west of the Euphrates; see Ezra 4:11), Zerubbabel son of Shealtiel, and the high priest of Jerusalem, Joshua son of Jehozadak. Both were Jews, permitted to hold office in the Persian Empire under the enlightened policy of local self-government which Cyrus initiated after the capture of Babylon. In the two years of conflict in the east, while Darius put down all opposition to his rule, hopes may have arisen in the west for still greater freedom from the control of foreign powers. If such hopes had arisen during the beginning of the reign of Darius, they had not yet crystallized into plan or action in Jerusalem.

The Unrebuilt Temple (1:2)

The first brief word from "the LORD of hosts" is simply a recognition of the uncertainty and hesitation of the people. "This people say the time has not yet come to rebuild the house of the LORD." The words of Haggai show no awareness of the elaborate preparations and auspicious laying of the foundation of the Temple described in Ezra 1:1—3:13. Nor do they specifically refer to the kind of discouragement described in Ezra 4:1-5. The popular attitude described in Haggai 1:2 suggests rather that the Ezra account is considerably overdrawn. It is likely that occasional small groups of Jews had gathered to make the return trip

from Babylon in accord with the permission granted by the decree
of Cyrus (see Ezra 1:2-4), and that as these exiles came, they
brought with them gifts intended for the rebuilding of the Temple.
The accumulated sum of these gifts during the nearly twenty
years that had preceded the second year of Darius can hardly have
been as great as is indicated in Ezra 2:69. The words of Haggai
indicate that no such wealth was available to the returned Jews
of Jerusalem in his time.

The Hard Times (1:3-11)

The next word of God which came by the prophet concerned
the people as a whole, not just the leaders. It asked, "Is it a time
for you yourselves to dwell in your paneled houses, while this
house lies in ruins?" Then it called for a consideration of the economy of the Jerusalem community. The people were reminded that
their bountiful sowing had produced only limited harvests, that
they did not have enough food to eat or sufficient clothing to keep
them warm. No savings were possible. Times were bad.

The remainder of this message is an explanation of the hard
times, combined with an exhortation to "go up to the hills and
bring wood and build the house." In the prophet's word the Lord
himself took the responsibility for the scarcity of material things.
"When you brought it home, I blew it away," he says. The reason
for this is simply stated: "My house . . . lies in ruins." This is the
explanation of a drought which has kept the earth from producing. The Lord was not pleased to see people busy building their
own houses while his was in ruins. "Build the house," he says,
"that I may take pleasure in it and that I may appear in my
glory."

GOD AND THE REBUILT TEMPLE

Haggai 1:12—2:9

The Presence of God (1:12-15)

With their leaders, the people responded promptly and effectively to the words of Haggai. Zerubbabel, Joshua, and all the
people obeyed God as his word had been voiced by the prophet.
The "remnant" may be understood as referring to the fact that
the people then in Jerusalem were but a small part of the once
numerous and great people of Israel, but it must also be under-

stood as referring to all the people except the leaders mentioned.

The opening sentences of the paragraph are concerned with a change of attitude which took place after Haggai's message on the first of the sixth month. At this point the people paid attention to the words of the prophet and took a more reverent attitude toward the house of God. Within three weeks the change in attitude took the form of actual accomplishment. No doubt much soul-searching and discussion followed the prophet's earlier words, and perhaps orders for the work were given by the leaders immediately after the first message of Haggai.

It was, however, on the twenty-fourth day of the month that "they came and worked on the house of the Lord of hosts, their God." This was apparently the day on which the foundation of the Temple was laid (referred to in 2:18 and in Zech. 4:9 and 8:9), the day, that is, on which definite construction began. What clearing away was needed may have been done during the three weeks after the first message of Haggai; it probably did not require the months between the twenty-fourth of the sixth month and the twenty-fourth of the ninth month.

No date is given for the brief word of God which came in connection with the changed attitude of the people and the beginning of their work on the house of God. It is nevertheless set between the reference to the changed attitude and the reference to the beginning of the work. It is a word of encouragement and assurance, "I am with you, says the Lord." Important as chronological data were to the compiler of the words of Haggai, the assurance of God's presence with those who hear and obey his words is of far greater significance. No glory can yet be seen in the Temple; no blessing is yet apparent in the fields; clothes are still thin, and the approaching winter will find many of the people cold. But God is present. This assurance the prophet can now give.

On what basis does the prophet make this statement that God is with the people? It did not come in response to something the prophet could detect about his fellows, but through the mysterious working of God with his chosen messenger. The prophet speaks because God has spoken. Thus the word of the prophet appears to come in response to a change of attitude on the part of the people, and at the same time it serves to motivate that attitude into action. The moment of its delivery is therefore irrelevant, and so also is the question whether the prophet was influenced by his observations of his people.

What appears significant is that with this word God accomplished his purpose with the people and their leaders. "The LORD stirred up the spirit" of leaders and people and they came and worked on the house of God. He was truly with them.

The Future Glory of the Temple (2:1-9)

Progress on the Temple must have been slow. Nearly a month after the day on which the people came to work at the reconstruction of the Temple, the word of the Lord came again to the leaders and people through Haggai. This message was delivered on the last day of the Feast of Tabernacles in the year 520 B.C., probably to those who were gathered in Jerusalem for the holiday period. It concerns particularly the people who were old enough to remember the former Temple of Solomon. Haggai's words invite comparison of the present efforts with the glory of the Temple which once had been. "Who is left . . . that saw . . .?" How does it look now? "Is it not in your sight as nothing?" The language indicates that some work had been accomplished, but that anyone who remembered the Solomonic structure would consider the present accomplishment either with contempt or with pity. We can only guess how far walls had been erected on the foundations, but it is clear that the building would be too insignificant to suit those who had remembered the earlier building. Haggai may have been one of these.

The message from God was, however, no rebuke; its spirit was not one of contempt or pity. It was a thrice-repeated message of encouragement, directed individually to the two leaders, Zerubbabel and Joshua, and to the rest of the people: "Take courage, . . . work, for I am with you . . ." The basis for this encouragement is the Covenant promise, made when God led his people out of Egypt, that his Spirit would remain in their midst. Exodus 19:5; 29:45-46; and 33:14 provide examples of the sort of assurance in Haggai's mind without using his exact phrasing.

The references to the past and present are now succeeded by a prediction regarding the future. "Once again, in a little while," the Lord promises to shake heavens and earth, sea, dry land, and particularly "all nations." The prophet's "once again" suggests a previous shaking of the realms of nature and of human government, such as took place in the crossing of the Red Sea by the Israelites at the time of the Exodus, but it does not exclude other more recent events such as the fall of Jerusalem.

The particular effect of the anticipated upheaval is that the treasures of the nations will come in, and thus that the Lord will fill his house with splendor. All the silver and gold belong to God, and it is his determination that the building now under construction will be more glorious than the former Temple. This new Temple will be rich and the people will be prosperous.

THE COMING BLESSINGS

Haggai 2:10-23

A Question of Purity (2:10-14)

On the twenty-fourth day of the ninth month in the same year, that is, in mid-December, a group of messages came to the prophet. Whether the messages are to be considered as two (as paragraphed in the Revised Standard Version) or as three is difficult to decide. The question is whether verses 15-19 of Haggai 2 belong to the message included in verses 10-14, or whether they should be considered as belonging between the first and second parts of 1:15. In either case the words of Haggai are so brief as to make the interpretation of the final section of the book difficult and somewhat uncertain.

Haggai's words on the twenty-fourth of the ninth month begin with a question for the priests. The question concerns the priestly understanding of the rules of ritual purity. The priests had no difficulty in answering Haggai's divinely guided questions. The mere possession of "holy flesh"—meat that had been set apart for use in the Temple or for the priests—does not give its bearer's clothes any power to make other food holy by contact. On the other hand, anyone who has become impure by contact with a dead body has the power to communicate his ritual impurity to any food he might touch. As the priests understood the matter of ritual purity and impurity, the one, ritual impurity, was felt to be communicable but the other was not.

Thus far in the text no difficulty is felt, but when Haggai applies the priestly understanding of purity and impurity to "this people" and "this nation" in verse 14, the reader at first assumes that the prophet is referring to the unworthiness of the people of Jerusalem. Then, if he seeks help, he finds that many commentators consider this to be a reference to the Samaritans and their desire to participate in the rebuilding of the Temple, as narrated in

Ezra 4:1-3. From Zechariah 7 it appears that contact with the
Samaritans continued during the reign of Darius, and it may be
that Haggai's message regarding impurity through contact with
the unclean refers to the participation of Samaritans in the worship being carried on at the Temple site. It is evident that "the
work of their hands" refers to "what they offer there," that is, at
the Temple. On the whole it seems better to consider that "they"
were simply the people of Jerusalem; the exact source of their
uncleanness is not clear from Haggai. Association with "the people
of the land" (Ezra 4:4), who had carried on a cult of sacrifice
both at Bethel and at Jerusalem, was without doubt coupled with
failure to reconstruct a proper house of God at the site of the
Temple. The precise cause of the uncleanness Haggai denounced
remains a question, but there is no question about the principle
which he enunciated. Impurity is easier to communicate than
purity. Is this not true in the twentieth century as well?

A Promise of Material Blessing (2:15-19)

Verses 15-19 have been understood rather widely as belonging
to the end of chapter 1. By promising, "From this day on I will
bless you," they serve to complete the contrast between the current hard times and the much desired prosperity. Again the
prophet explains the scarcity of material things; God assumes full
responsibility for the blight, mildew, and hail which have smitten
the products of toil. With the thrice-repeated word "consider,"
the prophet invites the people to note "what will come to pass
from this day onward."

In the ninth month, exactly three months after the beginning
of the work on the house of God, on the twenty-fourth of the
month, it was possible to see the prospect of God's blessing. Plant-
ing was complete; seed was no longer in the barn. Vine, fig tree,
pomegranate, and olive tree may still not have produced heavily,
but blessing was ahead. After three months of work on the
Temple, the people needed to be reminded that their plantings had
not been hindered and the necessary care of vines and trees had
not suffered. Again, the words of the text do not provide sufficient
background fully to illuminate the setting, but the prophetic message is clear: because stone has now been placed on stone and
the foundation of the Temple has been laid, God will bless. Action
taken in faith will lead to blessing from God.

The Establishment of Zerubbabel (2:20-23)

A second word of the Lord came to Haggai on the twenty-fourth day of the ninth month. This message was addressed to Zerubbabel and concerned his special position under God. Haggai at the opening of the message addressed him as "governor of Judah," but before long God's oracle described him as "my servant" and promised to make him "like a signet ring," explaining "for I have chosen you."

This brief utterance must be understood in connection with the divine messages, such as the fourth chapter of Zechariah, which suggest that the two prophets, Haggai and Zechariah, expected Zerubbabel to be established as the Messianic successor to David. The "signet ring" served as a man's signature; it was the instrument by which he accomplished his financial and legal transactions; it was the specific means through which he communicated his will to the world around him. As God's signet ring, Zerubbabel is seen to be God's chosen instrument of government. As at other points in the Book of Haggai the language is scanty, and the reader must use his imagination to fill in the details. Assuming that word of the victories won by Darius in the east had not yet reached Jerusalem in the ninth month of his second year, some commentators suggest that the prophets Haggai and Zechariah attempted to promote a rebellion against the Persians. It is more likely that the prophets simply expressed hopes for a divine intervention which would establish a Messianic king in Jerusalem.

Whatever Haggai's expectation regarding the establishment of Zerubbabel, his language sketches vividly the circumstances of divine intervention. It borrows from the figures of cosmic and political upheaval commonly used to indicate an intervention of God on "that day," the Day of the Lord. Heavens and earth will be shaken; kingdoms will be overthrown; military forces will destroy one another.

Nothing more is known of Haggai than appears from the brief record of his book. His contribution to the times in which he lived was the stimulation of his people to begin and to continue work on the Temple, and his spiritual legacy is the assurance that God will be with his people when they act in faith and obedience to his demand that he be given first place.

THE BOOK OF

ZECHARIAH

INTRODUCTION

The Man Zechariah

While there is serious question regarding the authorship of the second half of the Book of Zechariah, the first eight chapters of the book may quite properly be ascribed to the prophet Zechariah. Like Haggai, Zechariah is spoken of in the third person in these chapters, where his visions and preaching are described. He is designated as "the prophet" twice in the opening sections of the book. Unlike Haggai, however, Zechariah introduces himself into the prophetic utterances (see 1:8, 18; 2:1; 3:1; 6:9; and elsewhere), and appears to contrast himself with earlier prophets (see 1:4). No such personal references appear in the oracles of Zechariah 9-14, which will be discussed separately below.

In spite of the introduction of the personal references in Zechariah 1-8, very little can be said about the prophet Zechariah. His name means "The Lord has remembered," but this has no particular significance in his life and work. In Zechariah 1:1 and 7 the prophet is described as "the son of Berechiah, son of Iddo," but in Ezra 5:1 and 6:14 and in Nehemiah 12:16 no reference to Berechiah appears in connection with him. It is of course possible that the Ezra-Nehemiah references speak only of the grandfather and omit the father of Zechariah, but many believe that the reference to Berechiah was introduced erroneously from Isaiah 8:2 where another Zechariah is described as the son of Jeberechiah. Such a scribal addition to the text of the Book of Zechariah is quite possible, though no manuscript evidence for it has been found.

While it remains impossible to be certain who the father of Zechariah was, we know from Nehemiah 12:12-16 that he was a priest. From Zechariah 7:2-3, where the visit of the people of Bethel is described, it is clear that priests and prophets were closely associated in the time of the return from the Exile, and those who wanted advice and a word from God came to the Temple and its associated personnel for the answers to their religious questions.

While little specific information regarding the prophet is provided anywhere in the Bible, the discerning reader gains an impression of the man from the visions and preaching which bear his name. His sense of the presence of the messengers of God around Jerusalem, his zeal for the future greatness of the holy city, and his concern for its purity, all mark him as a prophet with a distinctive message somewhat more colorful than his contemporary, Haggai.

Zechariah's Ministry

Zechariah's ministry was contemporary with that of Haggai, but it extended at least to the fourth year of Darius (518 B.C.), when the emissaries of Bethel came to inquire about certain facts they had been observing. The three dates in the book mark the beginning of the three sections of the part which can clearly be ascribed to Zechariah, and appear to apply to the whole sections of the book which follow them. The date at 1:1 marks the prophet's first utterance, a general call to repentance (1:1-6), and does not appear to be connected with any external event.

The second date (1:7), the twenty-fourth day of the eleventh month of the same year (519 B.C.), appears to belong to the whole series of visions, though it is not essential to the interpretation of the visions to draw this conclusion. It has been suggested that this date marked the focal point of Zechariah's preparations in advance of the spring New Year Festival for an attempted coronation of Zerubbabel. During the postexilic period the Jews followed the calendar of the Babylonians with the New Year celebration in the spring, instead of the older agricultural calendar of Canaan with the New Year celebration in the fall, to which the Jews returned in postbiblical times. It appears likely that an effort to proclaim Zerubbabel as the Davidic ruler over Jerusalem took place in the spring of 519 B.C., though according to 6:9-14 the crown was placed on the head of Joshua the high priest and remained in the Temple instead of on the head of Zerubbabel. It is clear that any such effort to proclaim Zerubbabel as the legitimate king of Judah was abortive, and it is likely that the present form of Zechariah conceals the full extent of Jewish defection from Persian rule at this time.

It is also likely that the result of any such revolutionary ma-
neuver was the firmer establishment of the religious leaders in
power over the new community. In this respect it may be significant that Zerubbabel does not figure in the discussions of chapters 7 and 8 or in the account of the dedication of the Temple in
Ezra 6. By the fourth day of the ninth month of the fourth year
of Darius (518 B.C.), the date with which chapter 7 opens,
thought of rebellion against Persia appears to have been forgotten,
Jerusalem's prosperity appears to have been established, and the
prophet Zechariah was engaged in a discussion with visitors from
Bethel regarding ritual matters. The visit from Bethel, the occasion
for the final group of prophetic utterances considered to belong
to Zechariah himself, appears to coincide only with the onset of
the December rains and bad weather, but the fact that it took
place seems to indicate that conditions in Jerusalem were by this
time stable and prosperous.

Whether Zechariah lived to see the dedication of the Temple
in the sixth year of Darius (the spring of 515 B.C.), as described
in Ezra 6, is not known. His ministry appears to have met the
need of his time for encouragement in the face of the disillusion-
ing realities of foreign government, economic uncertainty, and
local apathy. To confront these realities Zechariah saw visions of
God, the Lord of hosts, returning to Zion to purify it and to dwell
in the midst of his Chosen People.

Zechariah's Visions

One distinctive feature of the Book of Zechariah is the occur-
rence of the series of eight visions, the heart of the material from
the prophet himself. These visions do not have the intensity and
force of the visions of Amos (7:1-9; 8 and 9), Isaiah (ch. 6), or
Jeremiah (1:11-19; 24). On the other hand, the visions of Zechariah are not as contrived or as involved as the visions of Ezekiel
(chs. 1, 8-11, and 40-48). For the early prophets a glimpse of some
object or setting provided the occasion and stimulus for a revelation from God; a momentary experience triggered the process of
insight in the mind of the prophet so that what occurred had the
intensity of "vision" and became organized around certain vividly
sensed words which were recognized as having the force of the
word of the Lord. In the experience of Ezekiel visions were less
spontaneous and became the vehicle for sustained presentation of

information, such as the detailed specifications for the Temple in chapters 40-48. Zechariah's visions fall somewhere between the spontaneous and intense visions of the earliest prophets and the sustained and complicated visions of Ezekiel and the later apocalypists.

Like the earlier prophets, Zechariah and the heavenly messengers who participated in his visions were concerned to interpret what he saw, so that those for whom the messages from God were intended should understand. In general, the meaning of Zechariah's visions is clear. They express the concern of God for the welfare of his people. The first three visions concern the future greatness of the Judean community, and reveal the fact that the normally unseen messengers of God surround it to protect it. The fourth and fifth visions concern the two leaders of the community, Joshua and Zerubbabel, and serve to assure each one (and the community as a whole) of the divine sanction for his position. The final group of visions concerns the presence of evil in the land and provides symbolically for the divine removal of wickedness from the land; the last vision provides assurance of God's satisfaction with the accomplishments of the other visions.

Angels, including "the accuser," the Satan, have a significant place in the visions of Zechariah. Though very much concerned for the welfare of his people, God manifests his interest through these heavenly intermediaries. God himself is observed to answer the questions of the angel and of the prophet, but the manner of his speaking is indirect, and he is present only as Spirit. By the Spirit of God, Zerubbabel will accomplish the task assigned him.

Opposition to God arises not only in men but also on the level of the intermediate beings of the visions. The Satan is one of these beings, a sort of "loyal opponent" in the angelic realm. Like the other intermediaries, he is in direct contact with the human participants of the dramatic scenes of the visions.

Zechariah may well have been led to use the vision form to present the politically dangerous scheme that appears to be at the heart of his messages. It is not clear today, however, exactly what he sought in the political sphere. He seems to have attempted to establish Zerubbabel as the successor to David in a genuine coronation ceremony in the partially reconstructed Temple. It may be conjectured that in a public address a week before the spring New Year ceremonies, on the twenty-fourth day of the eleventh month, Zechariah presented the whole series of eight visions, or the major part of them, to the assembled people. The balance of emphasis in the visions between Joshua and Zerubbabel suggests that what Zechariah sought was to encourage both Joshua, the high priest, and Zerubbabel, the governor, in such a way that they would continue to divide responsibility for the religious and secular spheres, while they brought their renewed zeal into closer subjection to the will of God.

Zechariah's visions thus provided a means by which purely political aspirations could be held to a minimum, while enthusiasm for the future of a community centering in the Temple could be stirred. Apparently Zechariah was successful in this moderately revolutionary program, for no immediate reprisals from the Persians were recorded. As matters turned out, perhaps not far from Zechariah's scheme, Zerubbabel did not become a center of real revolutionary activity, but power gradually became more and more centralized in the person of the high priest. The present form of the prophecies of Zechariah suggests that this was what the prophet wanted, but this may be due to later editing of his words.

The Oracles of Zechariah 9-14

While it is not impossible that Zechariah wrote the materials contained in chapters 9-14 of the book which bears his name, most students consider that these separately titled "oracles" are the work of other hands. The principal arguments for this conclusion are: (1) that the style and language are markedly different from the visions and prophecies of the early part of the book; (2) that at least some of the "oracles" of the latter part of the book assume circumstances which had not yet arisen in the early part of the Persian period, particularly the direct contact with Greek military forces referred to in 9:13; (3) that the religious ideas and mood of the "oracles" is different from the prophecies of Zechariah. It is clear that the materials found at the end of the book do not concern themselves directly with the events in the reign of Darius in the way the earlier materials do. Chapters 1-8 offer restrained encouragement in the face of difficult circumstances; chapters 9-14 look for the direct and vigorous intervention of God on behalf of his people on some none-too-clearly-defined Day of the Lord. No particular ethical demands are made of the people in chapters 9-14, where at the last everything will be "sacred to the

LORD"; in the earlier prophecies of the book, on the other hand, Zechariah has spoken in the spirit of the earlier prophets.

It is probable that chapters 9-11 were attached to the earlier part of the Book of Zechariah in the period of Greek domination over Palestine, following the victory of Alexander the Great at Issus in 333 B.C. Chapter 9 begins with a poetic oracle of judgment against the various Palestinian countries through which the conquering Macedonian traveled on his way to Egypt, and the remainder of this section of the oracles is concerned with the future of God's flock, part of it being composed in prose.

Chapters 12-14 are concerned with the future of Jerusalem and the Jewish state in some day yet to come when God is expected to intervene with destructive fury and to establish his people as victors over the other nations of the world. These chapters cannot be ascribed to any particular historical occasion but appear to represent the hopes of difficult postexilic times, probably during the Greek period.

The Message of the Book

As a whole the Book of Zechariah addresses itself to people who feel that God is not very close to them in the midst of their political difficulties. The first part of the book, particularly through the series of visions, declares that God is concerned for the welfare of his people, that his forces surround them as protectors, and that he will dwell with his people. Even when sin and its effects are dominant in the experience of the people, God purposes to do good for them. In the second part of the book, details regarding the nature of the divine intervention are set forth in the confidence that God will accomplish the purpose for good projected in the first part of the book.

Some of the details relating to God's intervention are of particular interest to Christians (see Zech. 9:9; 11:12-13; 12:10; 13:7) because of the way in which they have found fulfillment in the experience of Jesus. Other details, awaiting significant fulfillment (as, for example, in Zech. 14:8 and 11), have been further developed in the New Testament Apocalypse. But for the Christian interpreter some of the details (as, for example, in Zech. 12:1-9) have not yet risen to the heights of the spirit of the One who endorsed the great commandment of love to neighbors of all races.

The contemporary significance of the Book of Zechariah is not to be found through a study of fulfillment of details. Rather, through an understanding of the external pressures against which the expectations of divine intervention were set forth, we can come to recognize similar pressures in the world today. In relation to these pressures—some political, some economic, some social, all producing the sufferings men describe as evil—we must look ultimately to God for relief. Without adopting the particular programs set forth by Zechariah as the model for action, we must be ready for whatever action is laid upon us by the ever-present Spirit of God, who promises to accomplish his good purpose.

OUTLINE

VISIONS AND PREACHING OF ZECHARIAH

Zechariah 1:1—8:23

Introductory Appeal to Repent (1:1-6)

Like its companion and contemporary (the Book of Haggai), the Book of Zechariah begins with a date. Again in the second year of Darius, but now in the eighth month of that year, the word of the Lord came to a prophet. Thus the initial prophetic word of the book is, like the first word of Haggai, set in the year 520 B.C., during the unsettled times which followed the execution of the usurper Gaumata by Darius. Zechariah's word falls between the two dates given in the second chapter of Haggai (the seventh month and the ninth month), and appears not to be connected significantly with any particular event.

Unlike most of the prophetic utterances of Haggai, those for whom this initial utterance of Zechariah was intended are not defined. And appropriately the message is a general one intended for the whole people. Nothing in the introductory word indicates whether the people being addressed are in Jerusalem or Babylon or elsewhere, but other prophetic words of Zechariah concern Jerusalem and Judah, and it may be assumed that these first words also concern the city in which a discouraged and poverty-stricken group of returned exiles were being urged by the prophet Haggai to rebuild the Temple of God.

Zechariah himself is concerned with the rebuilding of the Temple (see 1:16; 4:9; 6:12-14), the future greatness of Jerusalem (see 2:5; 8:4-8), and the presence of God among the people (see 2:1-12; 8:3-8), but Zechariah's concerns are broader than those expressed in Haggai. The opening appeal for repentance shows clearly one of the major concerns of Zechariah. The substance of this appeal is blunt and clear: "Return to me, says the LORD of hosts, and I will return to you."

Zechariah did not concern himself with specific sins, but in this opening appeal for repentance he recalled the evil deeds of the "fathers." His people must not be like their fathers, to whom the former prophets preached. Because of their evil deeds before the Exile, the Lord was angry with his people, and when they did not respond to the preaching of the earlier prophets, they were wiped out, together with the prophets, according to the words of God. Only then did they repent and say, "As the LORD of hosts purposed to deal with us for our ways and deeds, so has he dealt with us."

This last statement, quoted from the Judeans of an earlier time, need not occasion any great difficulty, even though it seems a bit illogical to modern ears to hear a word of repentance from those who have just been described as refusing to repent, and to have a word from those who have been obliterated for their evil deeds. With prophetic and poetic exaggeration Zechariah has spoken of the destruction of the fathers. Actually, not all of the generation of Jeremiah's time was wiped out. Some survived in Babylon and in Jerusalem's environs and in Egypt, and those who survived learned the bitter lesson of the Exile, which is substantially summed up in this word of repentance: the Lord does deal with people as he purposes and according to his known laws and expressed attitudes. The fall of Jerusalem and the Exile had convinced a believing remnant of the Jews that God's expressed will would be effectively carried out. It is a lesson people of all ages need to remember.

Visions Concerning God's Intervention (1:7—6:8)

A Vision of the Lord's Patrols (1:7-17)

Verse 7 of the first chapter provides the second introductory statement in the book, in which the prophet's genealogy is repeated and in which a date is provided. Neither introductory bit of information is connected significantly with the substance of the first vision, which communicates the assurance that God has returned to Jerusalem and that prosperity will again bless his people.

The vision begins with a formula, "I saw in the night, and behold . . ." Unlike the pre-exilic prophets, Zechariah specifies that his vision was a nocturnal one. Daniel is the only other prophetic figure who specifically refers to night-time visions and dreams, and it seems from Micah 3:6 that the early prophets did not expect visions at night. Rather the moment of vision seems to have come to the early prophets together with the impulse to speak, so that the faraway look in the eye of the prophet was a proper accompaniment of the word of the Lord. Zechariah, on the other hand, received his vision, like Daniel, at night and arose the next day to present to the people what he had learned.

Zechariah saw a vision of a man riding upon a red horse; this man was standing "among the myrtle trees in the glen," against a background of other horsemen (presumably) on steeds of red, white, and sorrel. Whether or not "the glen" was a precise spot known to the prophet and his contemporaries has been debated by students. It may have been either the Valley of the Kidron, east of Jerusalem, or the point at which this valley joins the Valley of Hinnom, south of the city. Myrtles were common in these and other valleys near Jerusalem. In the prophet's vision the spot was only familiar enough to be described sketchily.

The significant feature of the account of the vision is Zechariah's discovery that he was in the presence of a sort of rendezvous of divinely appointed messengers. One angel talked with the prophet and answered his questions, promising an explanation of the other figures. The man among the myrtle trees answered the prophet's first question, explaining that his companions were those whom the Lord had sent to patrol (or to walk to and fro in) the earth. Then the angel of the Lord addressed the Lord himself and received gracious and comforting words which he passed on to the prophet in the form of a message for Jerusalem. Although God declares that he has returned to Jerusalem, he speaks to the prophet Zechariah only through an intermediary.

The message of the vision may be divided into two parts: the report of the patrolling riders and the gracious and comforting words of God. The report of the Lord's patrols is brief and concerns the condition of the world. Having gone to and fro about the earth, these heavenly police-like beings can report that all is at rest. This report must be understood against the background of uncertainty and hope which had stirred the peoples subject to Persia when Darius had killed the usurper Gaumata (or Gomates) in 522 B.C. Now, the patrols could report, political and military conditions had settled down and the earth was at rest. Darius was in firm control and the empire was stable.

The gracious and comforting words of the Lord have to do with Jerusalem and Zion, and they remind the reader of the opening words of Isaiah 40 with their emphasis on comfort, their specific concern with Jerusalem, and the direction to the prophet: "Cry out." The message of comfort to Jerusalem is concerned primarily with the attitudes of God and then with his plans for the city. God is "exceedingly jealous for Jerusalem and for Zion," and "very angry with the nations that are at ease." The "jealous

God" of the wilderness revelation (Exod. 20:4-6) who will not
permit the making of graven images has now directed his attention to those nations who participated in the chastisement of his
people. God was angry with his people—the sin was idolatry—
but the nations chosen to be instruments of his wrath had "furthered the disaster." As we know, nearly seventy years of afflic-
tion had been measured out, and during this time the Jews had
noted that those whom God used for the chastisement were also
guilty of idolatry, greed, murder, and the like—this is the problem of Habakkuk. The Jews had been assured that God had
measured double for all their sins (Isa. 40:2). Now an excess of
punishment has come upon the Jews, perhaps in the difficulties
they met in Jerusalem after the return, perhaps in the continuation of the annoyances of neighboring peoples around Jerusalem.

In the light of these conditions, four statements can be made to
Jerusalem: The Lord has returned to the city with compassion; his
house shall be built; the city will be reconstructed; and the cities
of Judah will again be prosperous. Zion (Jerusalem) will be com-
forted and again counted as elect. The vision is thus more explicit
than Isaiah 40-55 and somewhat fuller than Haggai in detailed
declaration to the people who were to rebuild the Temple. Such
daringly definite declarations can only be made by a prophet conscious of the majesty and exaltation of God and of his choice of
a particular people to do a particular task; this consciousness came
to Zechariah in his first vision.

Vision of Four Horns and Four Smiths (1:18-21)

Almost without interruption comes a second vision. The prophet
sees four horns. Asking what they are, he is told that they are
the horns which scattered Judah, Israel, and Jerusalem. Obviously
they represent those nations which had a part in the destruction
of the kingdoms of Israel and Judah, but they cannot be identified
with four specific nations. Rather the four horns stand for the hostility and power which completely engulfed the Hebrew states
from the four points of the compass.

This engulfing hostility is now in turn to be terrified and cast
down from all sides by four smiths. The smiths do not appear to
represent nations, and no further explanation is provided for them
by the angel of the vision except in relation to the function they
are to fulfill. In view of Zechariah's predilection for supernatural
beings, it is probable that he thought of the smiths as four heav-

enly beings, each corresponding to a point of the compass, with authority to destroy the political powers that had brought disaster to Israel and Judah. They thus represent the forces by which God would act to remove oppressive foreign government from Judah and Jerusalem.

Vision of a Man with a Measuring Line (2:1-5)

Again the vision changes, and Zechariah sees a man with the ancient equivalent of a tape measure in his hand. Asked where he is going, the man answers, "To measure Jerusalem, to see what is its breadth and what is its length." The meaning of this measuring is explained to Zechariah through a brief interchange between another angel and the angel who had been talking with him. Jerusalem is to be inhabited as villages without walls, because of the tremendous number of people and cattle in it. The lack of visible walls need not disturb the prophet or those to whom he will communicate this message, for God promises to be a wall of fire around her and to be "the glory within her."

To the people of Zechariah's time, the modern city with its suburbs extending in all directions without visible limit would have been incomprehensible. For them a great city must be protected by mighty walls, so that in time of war those who spent much of their time living beyond the walls might retreat for safety within the fortified area of the "mother-city." Zechariah could visualize Jerusalem as a city so populous that its dependent people could not be contained in walls. But although Jerusalem had no walls in Zechariah's time, the prophet did not envision the city as lacking in security. God would provide a wall of fire to protect his chosen city.

The glory within Jerusalem will be the presence of God in her midst, as symbolized in Ezekiel 43:4, and this presence will protect her from all harm. Zechariah's spiritual view of God permits only the protection of God's presence and the relative immateriality of a wall of fire. No warlike preparations appear in the background of his thought to disturb the assurance of the city of God's choice.

An Interjection: Call to Return from Babylon (2:6-13)

The first three visions have been concerned with conditions as they were at the time of the prophesying of Haggai and Zechariah. The Jews have begun to return; they are assured of the pres-

ence of God and of the future greatness of Jerusalem. Now, the
prophet interjects a special appeal to those who dwell in Babylon.
Addressing his kinsmen, particularly those in Babylon, but also
those who have been spread abroad "as the four winds of the
heavens," the prophet urges them to flee from the land of the
north and escape to Zion. The precise location of all to whom the
prophet addresses his appeal is not a matter of great concern, but
the reference to the north should be explained: the road to Babylon from Jerusalem went north, making a great arc around the
Arabian desert; along this road in the "land of the north" many
of the Jews may have been settled.

The word of the Lord declares that conditions will be reversed:
those who plundered will now become plunder; those who have
been serving—in captivity—will possess their masters. "He who
touches you," the prophet declares to the captives of Babylon,
will find that they have touched the pupil of God's own eye. And
the very nations who have "furthered the disaster" for God's people (1:15) will come and join themselves to the Lord and be God's
people.

In the manner of the rhapsodies of Isaiah 40-55 the word of
the Lord invites the daughter of Zion to sing and rejoice, declaring, "I come and I will dwell in the midst of you, says the LORD.
. . . And the LORD will inherit Judah as his portion in the holy
land, and will again choose Jerusalem" (2:10, 12). These appeals
to the exiles in Babylon agree with the message of the first three
visions as they point to the days of glory ahead for Jerusalem, but
they go beyond the visions when they include the joining of
"many nations" to the people of God. This idea, which is found
in Isaiah 2:2-4 (Micah 4:1-3) and Isaiah 56:6-8, distinguishes the
interjected exhortation of Zechariah from the visions.

Another feature of the interjection is the way in which the
prophet calls attention to himself, twice declaring that those to
whom his word comes "will know that the LORD of hosts has sent
me" (2:9b, 12a). Again in connection with promises to Zerubbabel (4:9b and 6:15b) this same self-conscious declaration appears. The expression is perhaps another evidence of the state of
prophecy in the postexilic period.

The appeals close with a word to "all flesh": "Be silent . . . before the LORD; for he has roused himself from his holy dwelling."
It is probable that the "holy dwelling" is God's heavenly home,
since the accompanying promises look forward to the re-establish-

ment of Jerusalem, but the words may derive from a moment in the ritual anticipating God's enthronement in the earthly Temple. This final call summarizes the evidence for God's renewed concern for his people seen in the first of Zechariah's visions, and invites the modern reader to be alert for a new demonstration of God's power.

A Vision Concerning the High Priest (3:1-10)

As though continuing from the reference to the glory within Jerusalem (at 2:5), Zechariah's next vision turns to the person of the high priest, Joshua, who appears to stand before the angel of the Lord with Satan (literally, "the Satan") standing at his right hand to accuse him. Again in Zechariah's vision word comes directly from the Lord, though only his angel is visible to the prophet. The word which comes is the familiar rebuke of Satan (see Jude 9), together with a rhetorical question in which God's rescue of the high priest is linked with his choice of Jerusalem. In effect, the question declares that in redemption Jerusalem is a brand plucked from the fire by the mighty redeeming activity of God.

Thus far in the prophet's vision the nature of Satan's accusation has not been explained. Now the angel orders those standing by, "Remove the filthy garments from him." And in words reminiscent of the inaugural vision of a young prophet in the earlier Temple (Isa. 6:7), the angel declares the removal of iniquity from Joshua the high priest and promises him rich clothing. At this moment Zechariah intrudes into the scene and suggests a clean turban for his head, and immediately the attendants provide it for him.

Now the angel counsels Joshua in a passage which contains a number of difficulties for the interpreter. The initial injunction calls upon the priest to walk in God's ways and to take proper charge of the Temple courts, and promises "the right of access among those who are standing here." Presumably it is this right of access to the heavenly council which Satan has challenged because of the inadequate clothing of the high priest and because this has been thought to indicate iniquity. Nowhere else in the Old Testament is it suggested that the high priest should expect the right of access to the heavenly council. Only rarely do prophets (Isa. 6:8; Micaiah in I Kings 22:19) overhear or glimpse a session of the divine council. But now, whether as a special promise to

Joshua or as the assurance of rightful prerogative, the sessions of the divine council are declared open to the high priest, provided he observes the moral and ritual laws in the conduct of his duties.

A second declaration to Joshua follows immediately, this time including his "friends who sit before" him. They are men of "good omen," and therefore the angel of the Lord declares, "I will bring my servant the Branch." These friends of the high priest are apparently his colleagues in the Temple, the other priests who have returned from Babylon with him. It is important that they should be included in the divinely provided approval, because some question of the fitness of all of the exiled priests had probably been raised, not only by the angelic Accuser but by those who had remained in Jerusalem and its environs during the Exile. The "good omen" attaching to the men probably represents the piety evident in their names. God recognizes their fitness because he sees their hearts, but their contemporaries may judge their piety by the names they have been given. Joshua, "the Lord will save," is a case in point.

It is significant that the priest and his position are dealt with first in the pair of visions which concern the structure of the post-exilic community. As Zechariah saw things, the priest and Temple and the removal of the guilt of the land were primary. The political area, signified in the announcement concerning the Branch and referred to in regard to hospitality under vine and fig tree, was secondary. In Zechariah's mind there was no conflict between Church and State, but the sacred sphere was his primary concern. God's first concern was with the ritual purification of the land; then he would provide improvement in its government in the form of the Davidic heir, the righteous king of Jeremiah 23:5 and 33:15.

The central problem in the interpretation of Zechariah's fourth vision is the "single stone with seven facets" upon which God promises to engrave an inscription. According to the text, the stone has been set before Joshua, not before the Branch. What sort of stone is meant? Can it be identified? Proposed identifications have included the underlying rock upon which the Temple was built (now visible as the "rock" in the mosque known as the Dome of the Rock) and the Temple itself. But neither of these can properly be described as having seven "eyes," and there is no indication elsewhere of expectation that God would engrave an inscription upon them. The divinely engraved inscription suggests the tables of stone upon which the Ten Commandments were written, and the stone with seven facets appears to be a jewel intended for the regalia of the high priest, either as part of the breastplate or as a pin for the turban. The inscription on the stone is linked with the removal of guilt from the land "in a single day," evidently the anticipated day of the renewal of divinely approved worship in the rebuilt Temple.

Vision of Lampstand and Olive Trees (4:1-14)

The fifth vision of the prophet is closely related to the fourth. In it he sees a lampstand of gold with a bowl on its top for the oil and seven lamps, each with seven lips for wicks. On each side stands an olive tree. Again an interchange of questions and answers with the angels promises to provide the interpretation of the vision, but before the interpretation is given there comes a special message of encouragement from God to Zerubbabel.

The special word to Zerubbabel concerns the task immediately before him, namely, the rebuilding of the Temple. In the form of a direct address to the mountain of rubble to be cleared away from the site of the Temple, the Lord announces that it will "become a plain." Furthermore, Zerubbabel, whose hands have laid the foundation of the Temple, will himself set the top stone "amid shouts of 'Grace, grace to it!' " A French translator appropriately translates the shout of joy as, "Bravo, bravo for it!" The special word of the Lord to Zerubbabel tersely declares, "Not by might, nor by power, but my Spirit, says the LORD." Zerubbabel may look forward to the accomplishment of his task, but his achievement belongs actually to the Spirit of God.

The interpretation of the vision points to the activity of the Spirit of God. The seven lamps are the eyes of the Lord, which range through the whole earth, instruments of the activity of the unseen God. The two olive trees, or the two branches from the olive trees, or the two golden pipes are the "two anointed who stand by the LORD of the whole earth." These two are also instruments of the activity of God, who is Spirit. The two instruments are men, evidently the high priest and "the Branch," understood by Zechariah to be his contemporaries, Joshua and Zerubbabel, the one pre-eminent in the sacred sphere, the other in the political realm. In both areas of human life God is Lord of the whole earth. By the Spirit of God the power and sovereignty of God are communicated to the life of mankind. Such explicit awareness of the spiritual nature of God's intervention in human affairs is seldom expressed in the Old Testament, but it became an axiom of New Testament faith as seen in the Book of Acts and the writings of Paul. It is a conception which needs to be rediscovered and re-examined in the modern world.

Vision of the Flying Scroll (5:1-4)

The final group of visions begins with the sight of a flying scroll —a huge scroll, approximately 30 feet long and 15 feet wide according to the prophet's figures. This vision and the one which follows it concern the purifying of the land and follow logically upon the divine establishment of the religious and the civil government accomplished in the preceding two visions.

The meaning of the flying scroll is made known to the prophet without formalities: it is "the curse that goes out over the face of the whole land." Thieves and those who swear falsely by the name of the Lord are particularly singled out as objects of the curse, which will "roost" in their houses and consume them completely. Like a huge bird of prey sent from heaven, the curse from God will destroy the homes of those who will not observe his Law. In ancient times curses were written on scraps of papyrus and delivered by the breezes into people's houses; this practice may serve as a parallel to this flying scroll from God. The thief and the false swearer will be "cut off," that is, removed from the postexilic community, probably by the direct effect of God's curse rather than by the action of the community. Moderns would ascribe such deaths to "natural causes," but the ancients saw them as the result of God's direct intervention in human affairs.

Vision of a Woman in an Ephah Measure (5:5-11)

The second of these two visions begins with an angelic invitation to look at something. Looking, the prophet asks for an explanation and is told that what he sees is an ephah measure (approximately three-fifths of a bushel) containing the iniquity of the land. When the leaden cover was removed, the prophet saw a woman sitting in the ephah. The cover was replaced, and he saw two women with storklike wings who flew away with the ephah and its contents to "the land of Shinar," the Hebrew name of the area between the Tigris and Euphrates rivers south of Babylon and known to secular historians as Sumer. There, the prophet was told, the ephah would be set down on its base in a house which would be built for it.

Clearly the removal of "Wickedness" from the land of Judah required a special intervention from God. It must be admitted that the special form this removal took in the prophet's vision is even more mystifying to modern minds than is the use of a written curse flying about the land. The representation of wickedness as a woman may be explained in part by the fact that abstractions in Hebrew are generally feminine, but it may also be influenced by evils associated with the worship of the pagan goddesses of the Canaanites, which had helped bring the downfall of the Israelite and Judean states. The house provided for the woman in Babylon, the home of wickedness, is clearly a temple, and in it the ephah and its contents would be put on a pedestal for worship. Thus the source of evil is effectively contained and removed from the land, as have been the particular evildoers mentioned in the previous vision.

Vision of Four Chariots (6:1-8)

In the final vision of the series of eight, Zechariah sees four chariots coming from between two mountains; they are sent abroad to patrol the earth, evidently to the four points of the compass, with the exception of the east—the desert region of Arabia from which no threats to the safety and security of Judah were visible in the time of Zechariah. The colors of the horses which drew the chariots are mentioned, but no particular significance can be drawn from these colors, except the observation that Zechariah was one of the relatively rare people whose nocturnal visions include color.

The "mountains of bronze" from between which the chariots issued cannot be identified with any specific spot in or about Jerusalem. Rather they appear to be a part of the prophet's vision representing barriers between the presence of God and himself.

At the conclusion of the vision, after an interval, the prophet heard the voice of the Lord himself crying, "Behold, those who go toward the north country have set my Spirit at rest in the north country." Again (as in 2:6) the north country represents Babylon, from which the Jews have been invited to flee and to which personified Wickedness has been banished from Judah. Only in the heart of the Persian Empire—in and around Babylon—has there been any serious unrest (in connection with the accession of Darius to the throne), and now God's Spirit has rested in that area. This means that the disturbances which God has caused in

Babylon in connection with the accession of Darius are now at an end, and the events of the preparatory period seen in the visions are accomplished: the religious and civil government of Jerusalem is established authoritatively in the persons of Joshua and Zerubbabel; evil has been effectively removed from the land; and the world is at peace. The era of blessedness for Jerusalem is apparently just ahead. Something like the Sabbath rest of the days of creation is announced in the final vision of the prophet.

Though God is not visible in any of the visions, his presence is real, and the accomplishment of his purpose is certain. For the contemporaries of Zechariah the voice of God was heard bringing assurance of security in a troubled political situation. For us the record of the visions brings similar assurance of security in the presence of the invisible God and in the certainty of his purpose.

Prophetic Preaching to Meet Particular Needs (6:9—8:23)

Instruction Regarding Crown and Temple (6:9-15)

In somewhat more conventional narrative form the Book of Zechariah continues with a word of the Lord concerning the making of a crown. The prophet is directed to take silver and gold from certain exiles who have arrived from Babylon and to go immediately to the house of Josiah, son of Zephaniah. Although four men are named at two points in the narrative (there are problems connected with the names of two of the men in verse 14), no further references to these men appear in Scripture, and the names appear incidental to the narrative here. The significance of the visit to the house of Josiah is not apparent. He was perhaps a craftsman to whom the actual making of the crown was entrusted, or perhaps he had accumulated funds for the furnishing of the Temple and the establishment of the proper worship in Jerusalem.

It is widely held by commentators that in verse 11, where the prophet was instructed to place the crown on the divinely designated head, the name of Joshua, the high priest, has replaced the name of Zerubbabel, "the Branch." Verse 13 requires a throne for the secular ruler beside which the priest shall stand. Between the two of them "peaceful understanding" shall exist. The whole prophetic utterance seems clearly directed toward "the man whose name is the Branch" (vs. 12), whose work will be the building of the Temple. The over-all picture of the times presented by Haggai and Zechariah indicates that this man, "the Branch," in whom Messianic hopes were then centered, was Zerubbabel. A later scribe, realizing that the expectations were not fulfilled in Zerubbabel, apparently made the change of emphasis which placed the crown on the head of Joshua.

The Hebrew "crowns" of verses 11 and 14 may be explained either as referring to the multiple linking of circles in the formation of a single crown or as referring to individual crowns for both Zerubbabel and Joshua. The final disposition of the crown(s) directed in verse 14 suggests that no royal prerogatives were actually assumed by Zerubbabel after the ceremony described in the passage—if indeed the ceremony was actually performed by the prophet. The crown was figuratively put upon a shelf, or "tabled," in the language of modern parliamentary procedure.

The final verse of the prophetic word is a promise that far-off Jews (and others?) will come and help build the Temple, if those who hear the prophet's word are faithful in their obedience to God. The blessings which God promises come to those whose faith manifests itself in obedient service.

Instruction Regarding Fasting (7:1-14)

"In the fourth year of King Darius, the word of the LORD came to Zechariah in the fourth day of the ninth month"; that is, in late November or early December of the year 518 B.C., nearly two years after the date of the visions, and two years before the completion of the rebuilding of the Temple. This word, unlike others in the book, came in response to a question raised by contemporaries of the prophet. As the passage is translated in the Revised Standard Version, the question appears to come from a group of visitors from Bethel. But the Hebrew text mentions no "people of Bethel" and refers rather to a certain "Bethel-Sharezer and Regem-melech and their men" who sent to inquire about the propriety of continuing the fast of the fifth month, which had been observed to mourn the fall of Jerusalem and the destruction of its Temple. The visitors arrived in the ninth month, which fact suggests that they had left some point more distant than Bethel shortly after the fast in the fifth month; their names suggest that they were Jews from Babylon.

The reply of Zechariah (7:4-14) is blunt and forceful and goes beyond the question raised. In the first place, the prophet's reply deals both with the fast which mourned the fall of Jerusalem in the fifth month and with the fast which commemorated the murder of Gedaliah in the seventh month, as briefly described in II Kings 25:25. Further, Zechariah's reply is addressed to "all the people of the land" and to the priests, as well as to the visitors; it is likely that the most careful observances of the fast were in the immediate vicinity of Jerusalem.

In and of themselves fasts do not please God. The former prophets had attempted to make clear the fact that God is not pleased by religious observances alone but demands right behavior. Fasts and feasts are of no real consequence to God, but serve the personal needs of those who participate in them. The prophet answers the visitors' question obliquely, much in the manner of the earlier prophets: whether the fasts of the fifth month and the seventh month are continued or discontinued appears to be of no concern to God.

What concerns God is the right behavior of the people: "Render true judgments, show kindness and mercy . . . do not oppress . . . and let none of you devise evil against his brother . . ." (7: 9-10). In these words the prophet summarizes the message of the earlier prophets, endorsing their exhortations as being of continuing validity, and goes on to say that the people of Judah had refused to hear God's Law and the words which the Lord had sent through his prophets. As a result "great wrath came from the LORD of hosts." The people were scattered among the nations and their pleasant land was left desolate. "As I called, and they would not hear, so they called, and I would not hear," says the Lord of hosts (7:13). The fasts of the past seventy years had been as ineffective as the preaching of the former prophets.

In this prophetic word the only gleam of hope is to be found in the reference to the seventy-year period. The inquirers arrived after the sixty-ninth commemoration of the fall of Jerusalem, and Zechariah's reply seems to have cleared the way for the discontinuation of the fast in the seventieth year. The construction of the Temple was apparently by this time far enough along for some limited use of it or at least for optimistic expectation on the part of the priests and people. God's hand had blessed his people, and now, if they will observe his laws and show mercy, his favor may show itself to them. The possibility of blessing is implied in the words of the prophet but not explicitly announced.

The Lord's Concern for Jerusalem (8:1-8)

A final group of prophecies ascribed to Zechariah begins with a promise concerning the future welfare of Jerusalem. This prophecy, together with the others of the chapter, is not dated and has no particular contact with the events of the reign of Darius. Its concern is the "great jealousy" of the Lord of hosts for Zion. The "holy mountain" is not merely the Temple hill, Moriah, but the adjacent hill Zion and the rest of Jerusalem with its other high points. To Zion the Lord promises to return, and in its midst he will dwell.

As a result of the blessing thus brought to Jerusalem, the prophet sketches conditions: old men and women will sit in the streets watching many children playing; people from east and west will return to live under the blessing of the Lord of hosts. Zechariah's picture is not as detailed or specific as that of Isaiah 60, but it is a picture of prosperity in which the burdens of labor will be removed from older people and from little children, so that neither group will be decimated by disease or forced to stay indoors at work. The basis for this glorious future is the presence of the Lord of hosts, dwelling in the midst of his people "in faithfulness and in righteousness." Can any community enjoy real blessing apart from the presence of God?

"Let Your Hands Be Strong" (8:9-13)

Following closely upon the promise that God will dwell in the midst of Jerusalem is a brief message of exhortation particularly directed toward the work of reconstruction of the Temple. It is addressed to those who have been attentive to the "words from the mouth of the prophets, since the day that the foundation of the house of the LORD of hosts was laid." The prophet contrasts conditions before the laying of the foundation of the Temple, when "there was no wage for man or any wage for beast, neither was there any safety from the foe for him who went out or came in." At that time God set every man against his neighbor, and there was no prosperity or security. Now, since the foundation of the Temple was laid (see Haggai 1:12-14), apparently in response to the preaching of Haggai and Zechariah, the Lord promises not to deal in the same manner with "the remnant of this people," the returned exiles and the faithful Jews who had remained in and around Jerusalem. Prosperity will begin with good crops as a result of bountiful moisture, and will lead to a reversal of status among the nations; the cursing and taunts of other peoples will become blessing. The message is addressed to both Judah and Israel, and evidently contemplates the re-establishment of the whole people as they had been under David and Solomon.

In view of the promise of improvement in condition which God will bring as he saves his people from the deleterious effects of internal strife, adverse weather, and the hostility of neighboring peoples, the word of exhortation is appropriate: "Let your hands be strong." God's process of salvation may not eliminate these external and internal evils completely or immediately; men must contribute their effort and must help in the removal of lingering evils. God saves, but men must build!

God's Purposes and Man's Duties (8:14-17)

The next declaration from the Lord could be treated with the previous section, for it builds upon the contrast between former times and the future. The fathers had provoked God to wrath, and he did not relent; now his people need no longer fear, for the same Lord of hosts purposes "to do good to Jerusalem and to the house of Judah." But the people have moral duties as well as an obligation to rebuild the Temple: they must speak the truth and render true judgments, and they must not devise evil or love a false oath. God has not ceased to hate the things that grieved him in the lives of the fathers. The people are under obligation not only to work at the Temple but also to build a moral structure in their community. So, though God purposes good for his people, his good intention for them is never held apart from the requirement of good behavior as set forth in his laws.

A Further Word About Fasts (8:18-19)

Almost as an afterthought on the matter of fasts comes another word of the Lord to Zechariah. Four fasts, including the two mentioned in 7:5 and adding the fasts of the fourth month and the tenth month, are to be turned into seasons of joy. The fast of the fourth month, observed on the ninth day of the month, recalled the breaching of the wall of Jerusalem by the Babylonians (II Kings 25:3-4 and Jer. 39:2-3). That of the tenth month, observed on the tenth day, recalled the beginning of the siege of the city by Nebuchadnezzar (II Kings 25:1). All four fasts, recalling the fall of Jerusalem, are to be made into feasts.

The concluding exhortation urges the love of truth and of peace, and suggests a proper mood for the celebration of feasts to replace the fasts. Incidentally, such a spirit is appropriate for all religious observances.

Pilgrimages to Jerusalem (8:20-23)

A final brief word of the Lord speaks of the future popularity of the Jews and of the way in which peoples will come to Jerusalem "to entreat the favor of the LORD." Jerusalem appears as a sort of Mecca for pilgrims from the neighboring nations; every Jew will find ten foreigners tagging along with him when he makes his pilgrimages to Jerusalem—all because the peoples of the nations, so unfriendly in the days of the Exile, have discovered that God is with his people.

Thus to the very end of the first section of the Book of Zechariah, we are concerned with the needs of people who cannot see God or hear his voice directly. In this last section it is no longer the Jewish people living in Jerusalem after the Exile, but foreign nations, who yearn for contact with God. Here, instead of angelic beings seen in visions it is the Holy City and the Jewish people who mediate the presence of God. Some mediation of God's presence is needed by prophet and Chosen People and also by the peoples of the world. What contemporary instruments mediate the presence of God to the modern world?

ORACLES CONCERNING THE PEOPLE OF GOD

Zechariah 9:1—14:21

Oracles and an Allegory on the Future of God's Flock (9:1—11:17)

Chapter 9 begins with the title "An Oracle," indicating that a distinct section of the book begins at this point. The word "oracle" is the regular translation employed in the Revised Standard Version for a Hebrew word "burden" when this word is used in the sense of a special message from the Lord (except in Jeremiah 23:33-40 where there is a discussion of the prophet's use of the word). In Zechariah (in 9:1 and again in 12:1) it appears as a sort of title, marking the beginning of anonymous prophetic utterances, the composition of which has been discussed earlier.

The Lord's Word Against Syria and Philistia (9:1-8)

The particular prophetic oracle or "burden" of Zechariah 9:1-8 is a word of the Lord against northern Syria, Phoenicia, and four of the five Philistine cities. The "land of Hadrach," mentioned in Assyrian documents of the eighth century B.C., was between Hamath and Aleppo. Tyre and Sidon had, through their cleverness, become wealthy as the centers of merchant shipping for the Near East, piling up money as graphically described in verse 3. Tyre had built her island fortress just off the Phoenician coast, and had successfully resisted Assyrian and Babylonian sieges, only to fall finally to Alexander the Great in 332 B.C.

Some regular campaign of conquest appears to be reflected in the oracle, even though, in typical poetic form, the cities are not named in precise geographical order from north to south. The oracle declares pointedly that "the LORD will strip her [Tyre] of her possessions and hurl her wealth into the sea, and she shall be devoured by fire." This sight will bring terror to the Philistine cities, and they, too, will suffer the consequences of defeat: Gaza will lose her ruler; Ashkelon will be uninhabited; Ashdod will become a mixed population; Ekron will degenerate from its proud status as an independent people and will become assimilated with the Judeans. But God will protect his house from the conqueror (vs. 8).

The identification of the oppressing king or general who will carry out the word of the Lord upon the cities of Syria, Phoenicia, and Philistia remains a problem for historians. It is just possible that the oracle originated during the eighth century, when Assyrians were campaigning across the Syrian and Palestinian countries (references to Hadrach and to the king of Gaza must otherwise be explained as anachronistic), but the oracle seems to owe its place in the Book of Zechariah to the experience of relief when Alexander the Great conquered Tyre and the Philistine cities but ignored Jerusalem in his haste to subdue Egypt and move on to the heart of the Persian Empire. The poet-prophet sees the events as the direct action of God rather than as a trail of human conquest. God's vengeance upon Judah's neighbors will be matched by his concern for his own people.

The Triumphal Entry of Zion's King (9:9-10)

The oracle continues with the familiar prediction of the humble but triumphant entrance of the victorious king into Jerusalem, quoted in Matthew 21:5 and John 12:15. In the second verse of the section the extent of the king's dominion is defined. Chariots, war horses, and battle bows—all accoutrements of war—will be cut off from both Ephraim and Judah. Need for these will no longer exist, since the king will rule "from sea to sea"; that is, from the Red Sea to the Mediterranean and from the Euphrates River to the southernmost "ends of the earth." Further, in the manner of suzerainty treaties of the ancient world, the king will lay upon surrounding nations the obligation to live at peace with one another. He will therefore arrive as a magistrate, riding upon an ass rather than a war horse, promising by this symbolic action just and peaceful government for the people of Jerusalem. With good reason the people of Jerusalem are urged to "rejoice greatly" and "shout aloud."

The entrance of Christ into Jerusalem shortly before his crucifixion was interpreted as fulfillment of the prophetic word of Zechariah 9:9 not only by the writers of the Gospels but also by the people along the road from Bethany into the Holy City. It appears that Jesus planned his entrance as a declaration of his role as the Prince of Peace. Like the borrowed ass of the occasion, the ancient prophetic word was waiting for his use. What the composer of the oracle anticipated is not so clear. Having reduced the enemies of the Hebrews to poor and ineffective remnants (9:1-8), the king could enter Jerusalem in triumph and "command peace to the nations." Some think that a scribe, observing the progress of Alexander the Great in 333-32 B.C., saw the fulfillment of an oracular fragment (9:1-8) and added verses 9-10 in anticipation of Alexander's peaceful entry into Jerusalem. The story that Alexander visited Jerusalem and sacrificed in the Temple is considered to be an unfounded legend, and certainly even the legend does not describe such an entrance as is sketched in Zechariah. Of unknown origin, the verses simply express the expectation of the coming of a "prince of peace" to Jerusalem, and for Christians this hope was clearly fulfilled by Jesus.

The Salvation of God's People (9:11-17)

Here further details of the anticipated victories of the Lord are elaborated. Captives will be freed from their pits, and restoration will be complete ("double"). Judah and Ephraim will be used by the Lord in attaining this victorious situation—against the Greeks

—and in the conflict they will be protected by the direct intervention of the Lord of hosts. In words which echo the song of
Deborah (Judges 5:4) and the prophecy of Jacob (Gen. 49:10-
12), the oracle promises that the Lord will "march forth in the
whirlwinds of the south" and that his people "shall drink . . .
blood like wine." Other vigorous figures of divine intervention
include "his arrow . . . like lightning." The passage closes in
somewhat milder vein with a promise that God will save his
people, since they are his flock. They will shine like jewels. "Grain
shall make the young men flourish, and new wine the maidens."

After the interlude depicting the peaceful entrance of the king
into Jerusalem (9:9-10) this part of the oracle, perhaps the work
of another hand, returns to scenes of battle and graphically describes the direct and forceful way in which God was to save his
people from their enemies, the Greeks. Only later than the time
of Alexander the Great did the Greeks become the enemies of the
people of Jerusalem. In its present form, therefore, the passage
appears to reflect the time of Hellenistic domination over Palestine
under the Ptolemies of Egypt after the breakup of Alexander's
empire. As in the earlier sections of this oracle, older poems anticipating the day of the Lord's vengeance on the world—such as
are found in Zephaniah—may have been edited so as to apply to
the current enemies of the people of Jerusalem and Judah.

The modern reader will be inclined to pass by the more bloodthirsty figures of speech in the oracle, but he should not ignore
the strong conviction of all of the fragments that God himself
would intervene to deliver and to provide government for his
people.

The Lord of the Weather (10:1-2)

In a brief fragment is found a command to ask the Lord for the
rains of March and April. Apparently arising in a time of internal political uncertainty—when the people "are afflicted for want
of a shepherd"—this directive is to be understood against the
background of superstitious consultations of diviners and dream-
ers and the offering of prayers to the household divinities known
as teraphim, such as are mentioned in Genesis 31:30-35 and I
Samuel 19:13-16. Regardless of the leadership in the community,
it is only the Lord who "gives men showers of rain."

The Future of God's Flock (10:3—11:3)

The reference to the lack of a shepherd leads to a denunciation against "the shepherds" of God's flock and then to a comforting declaration regarding the future of the two divisions of the Hebrew people.

The shepherds of verse 3 are evidently the leaders of the nations that have oppressed the Jews, probably the Ptolemaic successors of Alexander the Great, in view of the connection with other apparent references to this period. God expresses his concern for his people as opposed to the leaders, who may be presumed, therefore, to represent foreigners. These leaders will feel the fierce anger of the Lord, while he will enable his own people to "confound the riders on horses." The weapons with which God's people will defend themselves are the weapons of unequipped civilians: the cornerstone pulled from the wall in the emergency of battle and hurled upon the head of a luckless attacker, the tent peg (as used by Jael in Judges 5:26), and the trampling feet of a street mob.

Both houses of the Chosen People, the exiles of the Northern and the Southern Kingdoms (here described as "the house of Joseph" and "the house of Judah" respectively), will be brought back in triumph from the nations to which they have been scattered (Egypt and Assyria are specifically mentioned but not Babylon). They will be gathered to the rich lands of Gilead and Lebanon as well as to the central highlands of Judah and the hills of Samaria. There will not be room for them in the whole of the Promised Land. A new crossing of the sea or of the Nile will take place, and the people will be strong in the Lord. It is not specifically said that the two kingdoms will be reunited under one ruler, but only that the people will be many and that Ephraim "shall become like a mighty warrior."

The closing verses of the poetic oracle (11:1-3) turn in figurative language to the neighboring areas of Lebanon and Bashan, just mentioned as the principal areas to be populated by returning Israelites, and include a reference to the heavily wooded area surrounding the Jordan. But the emphasis in this section is not on the inhabiting of these areas; instead it is on the trees of each area that will be destroyed. The opposition to God's flock—designated here as the forests of Bashan and Lebanon and of the Jordan Valley, which were dangerous to flocks because of wild

animals within them—will be destroyed in the areas which will be
settled by the returning exiles. Unfriendly shepherds, lurking in
these forests to prey on the flock of God, will wail because their
refuge is destroyed. Thus in highly figurative language the poet-
prophet offers a basis for hope to the scattered Jews of the postexilic dispersion, as he sketches a land secure from the violence
and greed of robbers, whether these are robber nations or bands
of outlaws lurking in the forests. The goal of such security for the
whole world continues to be the hope of men nourished in the
tradition of human government under a righteous God.

The Shepherd of the Doomed Flock (11:4-17)

Following the references in the poetic oracle to hostile shepherds (10:3 and 11:3) and to the lack of a human shepherd for
God's flock comes a prose allegory in which a word of the Lord
directs an unnamed and undesignated person to "become shepherd of the flock doomed to slaughter." To this is attached a single
verse of poetry (11:17) on the same theme. Probably 13:7-9
should be considered as a displaced fragment of the same poem.

In the allegory the shepherd tells how he was directed to assume
his duties in the face of conditions adverse to the welfare of the
flock: buyers of the sheep slaughter them and go unpunished;
previous owners rejoice in the profit of their sales; and the other
shepherds have no pity on the sheep. Verse 6 interpolates a brief
explanation of the terminology used: the sheep are the inhabitants
of the land; the shepherds are kings; the buyers and sellers are not
identified. From the analogy of other dramatically communicated
prophetic oracles (as, for example, in Jer. 35 and Ezek. 4 and 5)
it would seem that the prophet himself was directed to play the
shepherd, to act in symbolic sympathy with and anticipation of
the divinely directed course of events. Here the prophet plays the
prince, governor, or king immediately over Jerusalem. The time
of the action cannot be identified.

Assuming his duties, the shepherd took two staffs, named
"Grace," or "Pleasantness" (the same word expresses "the goodness of the LORD" which the author of Psalm 27 sought), and
"Union," or "Binders" (suggesting the ties of confederacy or of
internal political organization). After declaring, "In one month
I destroyed the three shepherds" (who cannot be identified), the
shepherd explains how he became impatient with the sheep and
resigned from his charge, leaving the doomed flock to its destruc-

tion. As symbol of this action he broke the staff called Grace. Then, after asking for and receiving his wages he cast the money into "the treasury" (as corrected in the Revised Standard Version, see margin) at the word of the Lord, and proceeded to break the staff called Union. Then he was directed to assume the role and implements of "a worthless shepherd," that is, to be worse than his predecessors in the leadership of Jerusalem. The final poetic word of woe is directed to this worthless shepherd.

In the cryptic explanation of the allegory the shepherd's function was the breaking of the covenant of peace with surrounding nations (such as that mentioned in 9:10) and the breaking of internal cohesion among the remnant of the Israelites. Whether the expression "Judah and Israel" is to be thought of as the united Jewish community in the postexilic period or as symbolizing Jerusalem and Samaria at the moment of final break between the two religious communities is a matter of debate.

The thirty pieces of silver in the allegory are clearly the worth put upon the work of the shepherd by his employers, who incidentally have observed his actions and recognized that the word of God was being communicated through them. He is paid the price of a Hebrew slave (Exod. 21:32), apparently all his employers thought his services were worth. The casting of the money into the treasury may represent a deposit for safekeeping rather than a gift to the priests, but its meaning is enigmatic.

In the allegory the shepherd's hesitation in asking for his wages indicates that even he was doubtful of the value of his work. In the divine economy he has had an opportunity to be a good shepherd—to replace bad government with good. Even in the face of almost certain destruction (the flock is scheduled for slaughter), neither leader nor people could overcome human weakness and tendency to evil, and both internal and external political disintegration are the result. God therefore gives over the flock to the worthless shepherd, against whom he pronounces the final word of woe.

The parallels with events surrounding the crucifixion of Jesus can be seen; they consist of the thirty pieces of silver, the casting of these into the treasury, and/or the use of these for the purchase of the field of the potter. In the allegory these are incidental details. The shepherd of the allegory is not good (witness his impatience with the sheep), but he serves under a divine calling to be a good shepherd. This calling Jesus fulfilled.

The contemporary interpretation of the allegory must center on the calling to be good shepherds which comes to all officers of government. For officers of modern government, from the humblest local post to the most powerful world figures, it is not enough to affirm that Jesus was the Good Shepherd who gave his life for the sheep. Each person who assumes the responsibility for a part of the flock must resist the temptation to the corruption of his power and thus provide a basis for the continued welfare and security of mankind.

Oracles on the Exaltation of Judah and Jerusalem
(12:1—14:21)

With the expression "An Oracle" as at 9:1, the final section of the Book of Zechariah, composed mostly in prose, begins at 12:1. The section which ends at 13:6 is concerned with coming victories of Judah and with particular conditions in Jerusalem associated with these victories. The setting of these occurrences is in the future, "on that day" when the Lord will intervene to accomplish his far-reaching purposes, both for his own people and for the surrounding nations of the world.

Concerning the Future Restoration of Judah (12:1—13:6)

The oracle begins by referring to "Israel," but throughout it speaks in terms of Jerusalem and Judah. "Israel" is evidently a broad generic term for the postexilic remnant, and does not refer to the Ephraimite kingdom or its remnants. For reasons unexplained, "all the nations of the earth will come together against" Jerusalem and Judah, but "the LORD will give victory to the tents of Judah first" (12:7) and "put a shield about the inhabitants of Jerusalem" (12:8). The priority given to the clans (or chieftains) and tents of Judah has puzzled some commentators, but it appears that it was necessary for the prophet to maintain a balance of importance between those inside and those outside of Jerusalem. We may wonder if the author of this fragment was from a rural village.

Whatever the tensions between Jerusalem and the rest of Judah, the oracle graphically describes the complete victory of the combination and the devastating effects of the siege of Jerusalem upon the nations of the world (12:2-9). Contrasting with the frightful conditions of the battle is the majestic description of the Lord in verse 1, in whose name the inhabitants of Jerusalem and Judah will have strength for their victory.

A second section of the oracle (12:10-14) prophesies that on the house of David and the inhabitants of Jerusalem a spirit of mourning and of prayer will be poured out. The oracle emphasizes the bitterness of this mourning, its extent (the comparison with "the mourning for Hadadrimmon in the plain of Megiddo" probably points to the ancient pagan practice of ritual weeping for a dead god of vegetation), and the fact that the mourning will be carried out separately by families and separately by men and women within the families. This last detail is perhaps intended to suggest the depth and intensity of the feeling behind the mourning, showing that the participation of the whole people is not due to any mass hysteria.

The occasion for the mourning will be the sight of him (or "me"?) whom they have pierced. The pierced victim has been variously identified: as the shepherd of 11:7-14, as a prophet martyr, as a Messiah martyr, or as Simon Maccabee, murdered by the governor of Jericho in 134 B.C. (I Macc. 16:11-22). The Fourth Gospel sees the piercing of the side of Jesus as a fulfillment of this Scripture (John 19:37). In view of the piercing referred to in 13:3 it seems reasonable to assume that the mourning of 12:10-14 is to be for a prophet whose message was at first rejected. Later a deep feeling of repentance would possess the people, but not in the manner of a mass hysteria.

Chapter 13 begins with a single sentence which looks forward to the opening of a fountain for the cleansing of sin and uncleanness in Jerusalem. No particular stress is placed on the means of cleansing provided, and it appears that the oracle is concerned primarily with declaring the certainty of ritual purity for the people of Jerusalem in the day contemplated.

The final section of the oracle (13:2-6) foresees the cutting off of idols and the removal of prophets and "the unclean spirit" from the land. The initial declaration is followed by a series of comments on the removal of prophecy, which is an attempt to explain the prediction. Throughout the paragraph it appears that the rejection of the prophet is occasioned by the belief of his family and his friends that his vision is false and deceptive. The declaration of 13:5 is reminiscent of Amos 7:14 and implies that the author of the oracle wishes to dissociate himself from the low estate to which prophecy had fallen in his time. Along with this goes the underlying consciousness that he has spoken truly for the Lord of hosts.

At the time to which this oracle points—that is, in the culmination of God's purposes—Judah and Jerusalem will gain great victories, after severe trials. These victories cannot be identified with any historical battles, nor is it safe to spiritualize them into evangelistic victories for the Church. The prophet formulated his anticipation of military victories for his people which he expected to occur on the great and terrible "day of the LORD" (14:1). For Christians that day has become the faraway, but still imminent, Day of Judgment.

For the prophets the Day of the Lord was not usually the complete end of God's people. In the aftermath of the victories for Judah and Jerusalem the prophet sees a time in which religious feeling will be deep and pure, and the evils of idolatry and false prophecy will be done away. The symbolic language of the oracle is an effort to express the expectation of pure and refined religion in the day of the culmination of the Lord's purposes. Genuine revival can come only out of deep repentance and the putting away of the evils which God abhors. Thus for Christians the period of repentance and restoration is visualized as preceding "that day" rather than following it. Incidentally, Isaiah 61:2 (used by Jesus in the synagogue of Capernaum) makes the "day of vengeance" follow the "year of the LORD's favor." Real revival can come only as we recall that the sufferings of Christ are the means of a gracious outpouring of divine forgiveness and restoration.

A Further Thought Regarding Sheep and Shepherd (13:7-9)

A brief poetic fragment continues the theme of sheep and shepherd from 11:17. A sword is called to strike the shepherd, "the man who stands next to me." In some indefinable way this bitter treatment appears to be associated with the fate of the shepherd in 11:7-14 and of the unnamed person pierced in 12:10. Is this victim the worthless shepherd of 11:17? Again identification from the point of view of the writer is impossible. Appropriately, Jesus applied the reference to himself (Matt. 26:31 and Mark 14:27) in connection with the events of the Garden of Gethsemane.

As in the use made of the text by Jesus, so in the poetic fragment found in Zechariah, the weight of emphasis is upon the scattering of the sheep rather than upon the striking of the shepherd. The hand of the Lord will be turned against little ones; two-thirds of the people (as in Ezek. 5:1-4) will be cut off; the remaining third will be refined as silver or gold. The result will be a people of whom God can say, "They are my people," and who will willingly declare, "The LORD is my God."

The Coming Day of the Lord (14:1-21)

The final chapter of the Book of Zechariah is an extended symbolic picture of the coming Day of the Lord. It begins with a description of the terrors accompanying the coming day (14:1-5), describes briefly the security of "that day" (14:6-11), returns to describe the initiatory plague and panic (14:12-15), and concludes with details of the future blessedness (14:16-21).

Before the final blessedness Jerusalem will be captured by nations assembled in battle against her, and half her people will be taken into exile. Then will the Lord fight, standing on the Mount of Olives with such earth-shattering effect that a wide cleft will be created east of Jerusalem. Into this cleft God will come, accompanied by "all the holy ones." This picture of the final battle over Jerusalem (parallel to the account given in 12:1—13:6, but entirely different in detail) contemplates the actual personal participation of the Lord in the ancient manner of such battles as Megiddo (Judges 5:4), Mizpah (I Sam. 7:10), and others.

The prophecy looks forward to a time of "neither cold nor frost" but of continuous day (14:6-7). Neither the intense daylight of the Near East (with its heat) nor the damp and chilly night, but a condition like evening with its delightful breezes will continue all the time. A year-round source of waters will flow out of Jerusalem, dividing to east and to west (14:8). No ritual purpose is served by this spring (unlike that in 13:1).

The Lord will be recognized as King over all the earth, and no other will be worshiped at all (14:9). The prophecy contemplates the full acceptance of the ancient creed of Deuteronomy 6:4 by all peoples.

The geography of the Holy Land will be made over: from Geba, the northernmost town in Judah (near Bethel, as in II Kings 23:8), to Rimmon, probably near Beer-sheba, the land will be a plain except for the lofty plateau on which Jerusalem will be situated (14:10-11). Jerusalem shall dwell securely without fear of the threat of utter destruction in warfare.

Horrible plagues will befall the enemies of Jerusalem, if any are so foolhardy as to risk war against the divinely protected city. Disease and panic will overtake both men and animals, but the wealth of the nations will be collected—evidently as the spoil was left after the Syrians fled from Samaria (II Kings 7:3-15). The mention of Judah fighting against Jerusalem is a discordant note suggesting a persistent feeling of rivalry (found also in 12:2-5).

After the battles the survivors from other nations will come to Jerusalem to keep the Feast of Booths (14:16-19). This somewhat mechanical observance is viewed as the condition for rain upon their fields, except for Egypt which, being fertilized by the Nile, must be threatened with some other plague. The Feast of Booths (or Tabernacles) is important in this context not merely as the thanksgiving or harvest festival, but because it was the feast looking forward to the winter rains which were essential to the agricultural well-being of Palestine. It was also probably the occasion for the recognition of God as King over his people, and is thus appropriately connected with the recognition of the reign of God over all nations.

The prophecy clearly intends that everything in Jerusalem will be "holy to the LORD" (14:20-21). The Holy City will all be one holy area devoted to the worship of the Lord; the people will be free to use any available pots in boiling the sacrificial meal; no business transaction ("trader in the house of the LORD") will be needed to secure the necessary holy equipment for the performance of the ritual.

Like the oracle of 12:1—13:6, this final oracle of the Book of Zechariah looks forward to the day of God's victory over the enemies of his people and to the consequent blessings and privileges to be enjoyed by the inhabitants of Jerusalem. When we realize that the prophet was expressing the deep longings of frustrated and discouraged people living in a time when God seemed far away, we may understand his effort to sketch the conditions in which God would be very real and vital in the life of the faithful community. Our task is to make our common life "holy to the LORD" in the midst of our particular frustrations and to be aware of his rule over all things.

MALACHI

INTRODUCTION

Contents and Form

The Book of Malachi consists largely of a series of indictments of God's people based on imaginary questions addressed to God by the people. To these pointed questions the prophet addresses his replies in the name of the Lord of hosts. The whole series of discussions concerns the relationship between God and the postexilic religious community centering in Jerusalem—a relationship whose effectiveness and value the later generation of Jews began to question in practical ways. The actual questions posed by the prophet arise from the practices of his time and indicate the spirit behind certain abuses.

The only kind of division necessary for understanding the book is that provided by the questions and the prophet's replies to these. Only at 3:16-18 is the flow of rhetoric interrupted for a brief narrative statement of the results of the prophet's preaching, and this may be considered a parenthesis. The remainder of the book continues the somewhat extended reply to the question, "Where is the God of justice?" (2:17; 3:1-5).

The style of the book is not intense, but reasoned and argumentative. Each question raised by the people is stated in simple form, and its implications are examined. The reasoning is almost syllogistic, though as will be seen it frequently depends on a single specific instance rather than a generally accepted axiom.

The Author and His Times

For convenience the name "Malachi" continues to be used in reference to the author of the material contained in this last book of the prophetic canon, which is also the final volume of the Old Testament in the order commonly followed among Protestants.

It is generally agreed that the name Malachi in the title of the book (1:1) is drawn from 3:1 where the Lord simply promises the sending of his "messenger" to prepare the way before him. In the latter place it does not refer to the author of the prophecies in the book, but to "the messenger of the covenant" who is to come. The title appears to be, like other titles (for example, Amos 1:1; Hosea 1:1), an addition made by an editor, who attempted to draw from the book a suitable name for its author. Perhaps it was the editor's hope that Malachi had actually served the function of forerunner, and that the Lord himself would soon appear at his Temple.

The name Malachi means simply "my messenger," and, as it stands, is an unlikely name for a person. It may, of course, be the abbreviation of a name, Malachiah, "Messenger of the Lord"; this would be a proper and normal parallel to such names as Isaiah, Jeremiah, Zechariah, and the like, but there is no evidence for its use. The name Malachi has become fixed in the grouping of the twelve Minor Prophets by the scribal editor and has been generally adopted since before the Christian era as the last of the Twelve Prophets.

Though the prophecy remains essentially anonymous, there is almost no question of the individuality of its author. The book stands as a unity in form and purpose, and, with the exception of the last few verses (4:4-6), no part has been seriously questioned. These verses may be a sort of postscript added by pious scribes.

The author, to be known as Malachi for lack of any further identification, was clearly a thoughtful Jew living in Jerusalem, a God-fearing, patriotic man, who was concerned with the abuses of his time: the carelessness of priest and people with respect to offerings, the faithlessness of his people in marriage, and their lack of concern for widow, orphan, and sojourner.

The word "governor" (1:8) indicates that Jerusalem and Judah were in the period of Persian occupation at the time these prophecies were composed. This could mean any time after 536 B.C. and before the end of Persian rule. The only other reference to external events or situations concerns Edom (1:2-5), but unfortunately this cannot be used to date the prophecies accurately. After the downfall of Jerusalem in 587 B.C., the Edomites apparently swept into Judah and took possession of much that had been left; later the Edomites themselves were dispossessed. It is to this later dispossession that the prophet refers in 1:2-5. If its date were known accurately, a more precise suggestion could perhaps be given for the date of the prophecies.

It is not likely that Malachi's work came immediately after the ministries of Haggai and Zechariah, for the mood of depression and discouragement evident in Malachi must have taken some years to develop after the period of enthusiasm generated by the building of the Temple in 520-515 B.C. under Zerubbabel. In Malachi, the Lord's table or altar (1:7) is firmly established, the storehouse is available for the receipt of tithes (3:10), and the priests have grown careless with the handling of the offerings (1:6-8; 2:1-9).

Malachi was concerned with abuses. Nehemiah's reforms dealt with the same abuses: intermarriage with the people of the land (Neh. 10:28-30), tithes (Neh. 10:32-39), and the performance of the ritual (Neh. 12:45). Since no mention of a prophet appears in connection with the reforms of Nehemiah, it is reasonable to suppose that the prophecies of Malachi preceded the reforms of Nehemiah by some years. These reforms can be dated as beginning in approximately 444 B.C., and therefore the prophetic work of Malachi may be placed somewhere in the quarter of a century from 475 to 450 B.C.

This places the ministry of Malachi shortly after the battles of Marathon (490 B.C.), Thermopylae and Salamis (480 B.C.), and Plataea (479 B.C.). These events must have been reported and discussed in Jerusalem, but they did not concern the prophet. Though the defeats of Darius I and Xerxes I by the Greeks may have awakened hopes of freedom from Persian rule or expectations of Messianic deliverance, Malachi did not relate his prophetic thought to the movements of armies and the defeats or victories of military forces. His thought is almost exclusively concerned with the relation between God and his people.

The Message and Meaning of the Book

The Book of Malachi calls for the reforms made by Ezra and Nehemiah, and it is entirely lacking in the development of Messianism which came with the writings of the Greek period, such as the last few chapters of Zechariah. With reference to the successive codifications of laws, the guidance offered with regard to tithing is intermediate between that offered in Deuteronomy, the pre-exilic book of the Law found in the Temple in the time of Josiah, and that to be found in the priestly legislation, generally considered to be postexilic.

On the other hand, the message of Malachi is very largely in the ethical spirit of the earlier prophets, demanding justice, opposing false swearing and other abuses. Concerned with the correct performance of ritual as the earlier prophets were not, Malachi still insists on the inwardness of true religion. Like the pre-exilic prophets, he looks toward a simple but far-reaching visitation from the Lord in which those guilty of evil will be removed root and branch. The blessings promised those who are found serving the Lord in that day are general, as with the earlier prophets.

The message of Malachi was designed for a day of discouragement and disillusionment. He aimed primarily to persuade his contemporaries to take God seriously. If they changed their careless ways with regard to sacrifices, and if they took seriously the divine instruction regarding tithes, marriage, and the other directives of the law, then God himself would intervene in their behalf and provide overflowing blessing.

Malachi points the way back to a renewed clarity in ethical instruction as well as to renewed significance in the observance of religious ritual. The way back to significance in either area is through a renewed vision of the Lord of hosts, who takes an interest in the minutiae of human activity and who is the majestic "great King" who created us. Malachi's vision has its limitations, but it is sufficiently penetrating to enable us to see the importance of God in relation to our common life.

OUTLINE

COMMENTARY

QUESTIONS REGARDING GOD'S RELATIONSHIP WITH HIS PEOPLE

Malachi 1:1—3:15

Title (1:1)

The first verse of Malachi, like the first verses of many of the other prophetic books (for example, Isa. 1:1; Jer. 1:1-3; Hosea 1:1), is a title, intended to provide the reader of the book with the name of its prophetic author and some descriptive information regarding the contents of the book.

The book is characterized as an "oracle" or burden, the word frequently used by the prophets to describe their feeling of the weight and importance of the word of the Lord with which they were commissioned (see Jer. 23:33-40; Isa. 15:1; Nahum 1:1; Zech. 9:1 and 12:1). In Malachi the "burden" is specifically defined as "the word of the LORD."

All that the editor can do to identify the setting of the prophetic oracle is to describe it as addressed "to Israel by the hand of my messenger" (see margin). No specific date or reference to contemporary kings or governors is provided. Apparently the editor did not know exactly where to locate the work of this prophet. "Israel" simply refers to the remainder of the Chosen People then in existence.

Rightly, however, an editor separated it from the latter chapters of Zechariah, which are also designated "oracle" and are anonymous. Searching the contents of the oracle, and perhaps hoping that its author was the expected messenger of the Covenant of 3:1, the editor described rather than named the author of the oracle as "my messenger." Although the title in its English form appears to provide the reader with the name of the author of the book, it actually testifies only to the hopeful spirit of the editor of the prophetic canon and his sure faith in the divine revelation through the words of the prophets.

The Question of God's Love for His People (1:2-5)

The brief initial section of the book centers around a question supposedly on the lips of the people of Judah and Jerusalem at some time after the resettlement of exiles and the erection of the Second Temple. The prophet begins by quoting a word from God, "I have loved you." His quotation is not a directly literal one but may refer to Isaiah 43:4 or Jeremiah 31:3, or to the declaration of Deuteronomy 7:8, 13.

Opposed to this declaration of love on the part of the Lord is the spoken or implied question of the people, "How hast thou loved us?" Like the Pharisees and Sadducees seeking a sign from Jesus, the people of Malachi's day cannot see clear and unmistakable evidences of the love of God. Like some contemporary thought, which fears to speak of God or moral values because it cannot see these in any tangible form, the central question of the prophet's day only probed in the direction of ultimate realities. The inhabitants of Jerusalem were not so sophisticated as to question the existence of God, but they could ask—by action if not in word—whether God was showing his love for his people in a tangible way.

A single instance is all that is required to refute an argument which might otherwise end in a universal negative. Malachi answers the question with an illustration from what was apparently a contemporary event. In the personifying language of his time, he asks, "Is not Esau Jacob's brother?" and continues, "Yet I have loved Jacob but I have hated Esau." More precisely he goes on to explain that what has happened to the hill country of Edom (Esau) is clear evidence that God cares more for Judah than he does for the neighbor people whose home was across the Dead Sea southeast of Judah.

The chronology of events to which Malachi refers is not known accurately, but the sequence is generally recognized. During the siege of Jerusalem and after its fall in 587 B.C., the Edomites not only failed to help the Jews but apparently rejoiced in their downfall (Lam. 4:21-22; Ps. 137:7) and rushed in to collect spoil. Later, perhaps in the period immediately preceding Malachi's prophetic ministry, the Nabataean Arabs in turn seized the hill country of Edom and drove the Edomites westward into the southern section of Judah, where ultimately their descendants set up the Idumaean kingdom with its capital at Hebron. Malachi seems to be referring to the desolation left by the flight of the Edomites from their native lands. This destruction is from God, and no efforts to rebuild will avail. The desolate country will be a continuing monument to the vengeance God brought upon the heads of those who had turned their backs upon his people in their day of trouble.

As the Jews look beyond their borders, they may be continually reminded of the greatness of the Lord, whose avenging power is able to destroy a former kinsman turned bitter enemy. It is in this willingness to avenge the injury done his people that God's love was manifested. With a wider vision of history the contemporary Christian should be able to provide himself with far more satisfactory evidences of the love of God (see also Rom. 9:13-18).

The Question of Proper Respect for God (1:6—2:9)

The next section of Malachi's argument with his contemporaries is addressed primarily to the priests, since they are responsible for the conduct of worship, but it concerns also the offerings actually presented by the people.

Malachi begins by stating what was axiomatic in his day, "A son honors his father, and a servant his master." In a "how much more" deduction from this premise, Malachi raises the question for the Lord, "If then I am a father, where is my honor?" Then, turning to the priests, the prophet addresses them as those "who despise my name." Again, their question—uttered or implied— forms the basis for an exposition of the abuses of the ritual current in that day.

Priests and people have despised the name of the Lord "by offering polluted food" on God's altar. They have polluted the offerings "by thinking that the LORD's table may be despised." Malachi is not arguing in a circle, for he continues with specific charges: the people, led by their priests, have brought blind, lame, and sick animals as their sacrifices. The law required perfect animals; no blemished animal was to be presented to God (Deut. 15:21). Some even went further: they vowed to present an unblemished male from their flock, but then presented a blemished substitute (1:14).

Much of the first paragraph of this lengthy indictment (1:6-14) is addressed to the layman, who should be able to see how his behavior has been contemptuous of God. "Present that to your governor," says the prophet in the name of God; "will he be pleased with you or show you favor?" Genuine respect should result in the presentation of the best sort of gifts; even self-interest prompts people to present acceptable gifts to the politically powerful.

Interrupting his bill of particulars, the prophet looks in vain for "one . . . who would shut the doors, that you might not kindle fire upon my altar in vain!" No sacrifice at all would be preferable to the blemished offerings that have been presented.

In this connection the prophet makes the most striking statement of all (1:11), declaring that from east to west, "in every place," the name of God is great among the nations and incense and a pure offering are offered to the name of God. It is clear that Malachi has a high view of God as "a great King" (1:14), but the idea that God accepts any conscientiously offered sacrifice is unexpected, to say the least. Such universalism is not elsewhere expressed in the Bible, though at many points in the prophetic writings of the Old Testament the idea of the participation of non-Jews in the worship of God is expressed (see, for example, Isa. 2:2-3 and Zech. 14:16). Malachi's statement is as broad as that of the author of the Letter to the Hebrews (11:6), "Whoever would draw near to God must believe that he exists and that he rewards those who seek him," but it is more specific in including the worship of pagans. Taken in its context with reference to the necessity for due respect to God, it may be understood as other prophetic hyperboles are understood: blemished Jewish sacrifices are not acceptable; pagan sacrifices, conscientiously offered, are far more acceptable. The statement may offer some clue to the beginnings of Jewish proselytism in the period between the Old and New Testaments. As thoughtful pagans began to repudiate the more sensual and polytheistic elements of their traditional beliefs, it became possible for Jews to consider them as proselytes, or, as in the case of Malachi, to see them as sharing essentially the same faith. Malachi's view of such pagans, however, did not prevail.

Malachi's indictment turns to the priests and in a strongly worded paragraph (2:1-9) threatens them with disgrace before the people and exclusion from the presence of God. Their offerings will be cursed, in fact, have already been cursed; their offspring will be rebuked; the dung of offerings will be spread on their faces. The reason is at first simply stated: "If you will not listen, if you will not . . . give glory to my name." Later, the prophet adds another explanation: "Inasmuch as you have not kept my ways but have shown partiality in your instruction."

Instruction is the Hebrew word, Torah, or Law, used here in its simplest sense. Instruction was the priest's specific guidance to the individual worshiper, an example of which appears in Deuteronomy 26:1-15. It was the duty of the priest to assist in the performance of rituals, to see to it that the worshiper said the right words (Deut. 26), and to see that the animal was killed in the right way, as in the later laws recorded in Leviticus 1:1-17. Any such direct guidance provided the worshiper by the priest was "instruction." It was this which the priests of Malachi's time had perverted.

Malachi contrasts the present ministry of the priests with that of a somewhat idealized Levi, the ancestor of the priests and the Levites. According to Malachi's picture the Lord had made a covenant with Levi, promising life and peace if he "feared" God. Here Levi did actually "fear" the Lord; that is, he spoke true instruction, and no wrong was upon his lips. By this instruction the idealized Levi "turned many from iniquity" and walked with God in peace and uprightness. Peace should be understood in this context as referring to wholeness or its modern near equivalent, "integrity." Levi was, according to this view of him, a true messenger of the Lord to his generation, instructing wisely and serving as an ideal priest.

The covenant with Levi alluded to in this ideal sketch is not clearly defined in the Old Testament. In Numbers 25:10-13 (and Ps. 106:30-31) a covenant with Phinehas, the grandson of Aaron, is mentioned in connection with his zeal for the Lord during the religious debacle at Peor when the Israelites sacrificed to Baal with the Moabites. Deuteronomy 33:8-11 may refer to the same incident, but there Levi stands for the priestly tribe, and the setting is at Massah and the waters of Meribah. The bitterness expressed against Levi in Genesis 49:5-7 has been entirely forgotten in the blessing of Moses in Deuteronomy (33:8-11) and in Malachi's words. In Malachi's idealized picture, Levi is the representative of the priestly tribe. Evidently Malachi transferred the recollection of the incident with Phinehas and the establishment of a special covenant with him to his tribal ancestor, Levi. To this ideal from the ancient past the contemporary priests have not been true. Being the recognized leaders of Malachi's day, the priests had a heavy responsibility and deserved severe rebuke and punishment for their faithlessness.

The Question of General Faithfulness (2:10-16)

Turning from the priests to the people as a whole, Malachi

raises the question of faithfulness in regard to two specific areas: first with regard to the worship of false gods and then with regard to marriage vows. Beginning again with an axiomatic statement expressed as a pair of rhetorical questions, he affirms the unity of his people under the creative action of God. "Why then," he asks, "are we faithless to one another, profaning the covenant of our fathers?" Earlier prophets would have stressed the ethical failures of the time (for example, false swearing, oppression, to which Malachi does refer in 3:5), but at this point Malachi is still concerned with the proper worship of the Lord. "Judah has profaned the sanctuary of the LORD." "He . . . has married the daughter of a foreign god," says the prophet. This does not refer to mixed marriages among the people, but to participation in pagan rituals. Malachi does not provide any more specific information regarding such pagan rituals, and it is not clear that they were actually performed in the Temple. Perhaps he had in mind household customs brought into the life of the Jewish people through their mixed marriages. Whatever the precise way in which the people had been faithless, Malachi calls down a curse upon those who were guilty: May the Lord eliminate the family of any man who is faithless, so that his family will have no representative in community gatherings or in the presentation of offerings to the Lord!

The second area (2:13-16) in which Malachi's contemporaries had proved faithless was in relation to their wives. Again Malachi approaches his thought indirectly, this time observing that the people are weeping and groaning at the altar because God does not accept their offerings. Why not? "Because the LORD was witness to the covenant between you and the wife of your youth, to whom you have been faithless." The prophet proceeds to present the Old Testament doctrine of marriage in its highest form, pointing to its nature as a covenant relationship sanctioned by God, intended to provide for companionship and for the procreation of godly offspring.

God, says the prophet, hates divorce. Twice Malachi exhorts the people to take heed and not to be faithless in this important area. Monogamy appears to be assumed as normal; polygamy is not a permissible alternative in the postexilic period. Divorce, as the way out of a relationship which the husband feels to be undesirable, is to cover "one's garment with violence," according to Malachi. This last expression appears to refer to the custom of throwing a cloak over a woman as a sign of protection or of willingness to marry her, as in Ruth 3:9. In Malachi's time, however, the men of Jerusalem apparently were divorcing their wives after years of marriage and taking younger women, perhaps from the surrounding pagan peoples. But this was to do violence to the covenant relationship sanctioned by God, and to injure the legitimate wife.

The Question of the Reality of God's Judgment (2:17—3:5)

From Malachi's point of view, seeing conditions as God sees them, it is obvious why the Lord does not show favor to the offerings of people who are guilty of such contempt for God and such faithlessness as he has described. No amount of "weeping and groaning" at the altar (2:13) could remedy the defect in the personal character of the Jews of Jerusalem.

God has become weary of the words of the people (2:17). It is easy to see here a projection of the feelings of the people (comparing 1:13 with 2:17): they have felt weary of the ritual of sacrifice; God himself must be weary. But the prophet declares: the people have wearied God by saying (in actions, perhaps, rather than words), "Everyone who does evil is good in the sight of the LORD, and he delights in them." It seemed that God took no thought of relative goodness or evil. Or, expressed in another way, the people were wondering, "Where is the God of justice?" When evil seems to prosper without restraint, when pious men find no reality in worship and are content to offer less than their best to God, the reality of God's judgment is called in question. God either does not see the abuses or he does not care. The question was not new with Malachi (for example, see Hab. 1:2-4), and it remains relevant in every age.

As Malachi's question is oriented toward the ritual of public worship, so the answer provided through him is related to the coming of the Lord to his Temple (3:1-5). The coming of the Lord will be preceded, as was proper in the processions by which oriental monarchs approached their thrones, by the arrival of an advance messenger. The messenger will "sit as a refiner and purifier of silver" (see an earlier prophet's use of the figure in Jer. 6:27-30), purifying the tribe of Levi until they offer sacrifices which God can accept. Then the offering of Judah and Jerusalem will again be acceptable to the Lord as it was in ancient times, perhaps as far back as the idealized period following the episode at Peor, to which the prophet has apparently referred in 2:4-7

(see Num. 25:10-13). Not only the ritual of the cult will be purified, but also the social behavior of the people; verse 5 pronounces
a judgment against sorcerers, adulterers, false swearers, and oppressors of the weak. Beginning at the house of God, the judgment of the messenger of the covenant will purify the whole life
of the people.

The effects of the promised divine visitation are thus clear
enough. None can endure its arrival; priests will be first to be
affected, but all others will be reached. Purification will be the
order of the day. The consuming effects of the visitation are not
mentioned here, but they are at 4:1; the important consequence
is the re-establishment of an offering pleasing to the Lord. Protes-
tant scholars deny the Roman Catholic view that this prophesies
the establishment of the Mass, but they have provided little con-
structive interpretation to take the place of this idea. Actually
Malachi does not look ahead as far as the Christian era, but only
to a time when a proper worship of God will be central in Jerusalem and offered by a people who fear the Lord and who do not
disobey his commands. The Christian equivalent is a community
where worship is central and vital and where social relationships
are animated by the high ethics of the Sermon on the Mount.

The problem of the identity of the messenger and of his relationship to the Lord has vexed interpreters from the time of the
editor of the book to the present day. The editor of the book appears to have believed that the looked-for messenger was the
prophet himself; an annotator (4:5) seems to have thought that
Elijah would be brought back to earth to be the messenger of the
Covenant. Mark (1:2) and the early Christian community believed that John the Baptist was the expected messenger. It is
probable that the writer of the prophecy thought only of the messenger who announced the coming of a royal personage, to be
seen by the populace. The messenger is thus an agent, representing the coming of the Lord to his Temple, rather than a particular historical person. The prophet may have expected a priest to
accomplish the reformation in the Temple, since his earlier ideal-
ization of Levi suggests the kind of messenger he would have
approved.

But the Lord's place in the expectation of Malachi must be
considered. The messenger of the Covenant is closely related to
the Lord himself, so closely related that it is difficult to determine
whether God himself performs the cleansing function. It is clear

that the traditional Davidic Messianic figure does not appear; instead, the direct intervention of the Lord himself is all that can be seen. Malachi's expectations cannot be defined further, and it is unlikely that he had precise ideas of future events. Using expressions of the effects of the coming of the Lord similar to those of the earlier prophets, Malachi brought to his time a new sense of the reality of divine judgment.

The Question of Returning to God (3:6-12)

Malachi's next section deals with the proper handling of tithes, but he sees these as a means by which the people may escape the consuming judgment of God. The prophet begins by declaring that the Lord does not change. Because of God's unchanging concern the people have not yet been destroyed, in spite of their ritual abuses and moral perversity. In the spirit of the pre-exilic prophets Malachi invites a return to the Lord of hosts.

"How shall we return?" the people appear to ask, and the prophet proceeds to his indictment. The inconceivable is happening: the people are robbing God! A curse rests on the whole nation because all have been robbing God in the handling of tithes and offerings. The prophet indicates the specific particulars of his indictment in a direct command, "Bring the full tithes into the storehouse, that there may be food in my house." It is possible to see the situation through these words. Tithes have been kept at home, presumably until times are better or are more convenient for delivery to the Temple storehouse; now the storehouse from which priests were supposed to be fed is practically empty. As a result, says the prophet, "the devourer," perhaps a locust swarm, has been abroad in the land, destroying the fruit of vines and fields. But if the people return by responding to the call for the tithe, the Lord promises to "open the windows of heaven . . . and pour down . . . an overflowing blessing." Malachi takes his stand with the traditional reward-and-punishment view of God's action, as this is expressed in the blessings and curses of Deuteronomy. With Malachi the reward for proper presentation of tithes and offerings is primarily material. It is not necessarily so for us, however, though many tithers insist that material blessings have followed the initiation of serious and careful setting apart of at least the tenth for the Lord.

In the generally nationalistic frame of Malachi's thought, it is of interest to note one special reward mentioned in connection with the bringing of the tithes to God. "All nations will call you blessed" (3:12). Malachi's question, "Will man rob God?"—like the statement of 1:11 regarding acceptable pagan worship—refers to the human race as a whole. Malachi's view sees God's own people as peculiarly guilty in the light of their knowledge of God's will through the traditional instruction of the priests. Other nations are ready to bless God, and are even capable of offering sacrifice which is acceptable to God; they would not think of robbing God! Malachi's words provide a preface to a theology of world missions somewhat different from the traditional "rescue the perishing" view. With this prophet God's call is to the elect community to be faithful to his command, so that the ensuing blessing will attract the attention of interested pagans.

The Question of Speaking Against God (3:13-15)

In a brief paragraph Malachi returns to an idea he has already expressed (2:17). Replying to the question, "How have we spoken against thee?" Malachi tells his people that they have said, "It is vain to serve God." In the mood of disillusionment of the times, even the pious have been tempted to give up the effort to obey the commandments or to walk "as in mourning before the LORD of hosts." Having raised this question, Malachi simply leaves it unanswered. The kind of answer he would have given, and perhaps did give, is obvious. Or perhaps by this time his message was interrupted by the action described in 3:16. Some of the people, at least, saw that their actions, if not their words, had been against God.

CONCLUDING NARRATIVE AND FURTHER DECLARATIONS

Malachi 3:16—4:6

The Book of Remembrance for Those Who Feared (3:16-18)

In the single verse of narrative (3:16) contained in the Book of Malachi it is reported that "those who feared the LORD spoke with one another; the LORD heeded and heard them, and a book of remembrance was written before him of those who feared the LORD and thought on his name." The remainder of the brief paragraph quotes God as declaring that those whose names were entered in the book of remembrance will be his special possession on the day when he acts, to be spared as a father spares a faithful son. Then, the prophet adds, "you shall distinguish between the righteous and the wicked, between one who serves God and one who does not serve him."

This experience of the prophet is not described as a vision, but clearly it involves something of the special powers of insight into divine reality which were the mark of the prophets. The attached prophetic word appears to contemplate an immediate action of God of such definite judgment as to make clear to all the difference "between the righteous and the wicked."

The Coming Day of the Lord (4:1-3)

Malachi's view of that day of direct intervention by God is further developed in the short paragraph which follows. It is characterized in terms of the heat of an oven which is capable of destroying "the arrogant and all evildoers" like stubble. Those who fear the name of the Lord, that is, who attend to his commands, will go forth "leaping like calves from the stall," and will tread down the wicked, evidently sharing in the consuming activity of God, since these latter will be left as "ashes under the soles of your feet."

Malachi does not have a fully developed sequence of events in mind for the end of time; rather he contemplates an imminent catastrophe for the wicked of his own time from which the conscientious worshipers of the Lord will be saved and in which they will have a part. The idea of the participation of the righteous in the judgment of the wicked appears in a variety of forms in the Old Testament, often (as in Amos 9:12 and Isa. 11:13-14) involving only the repossession by Israel of territory conquered by her neighbors. Micah (4:13) sees his people as the divinely authorized threshing instrument which God will use against "many peoples." Malachi's idea that righteous Jews will turn against their fellow Jews is not found elsewhere in the Old Testament.

Christians have come to see the participation of God's elect in the fulfillment of his purposes through missionary activity and, with a more developed view of the end of the world, have come to think of the catastrophic separation of righteous from wicked as a phase of the Last Judgment. What is particularly relevant in all of these views, which need not be harmonized with each other, is the conception of divine disapproval upon evil, and the promise of God's blessing upon those who show proper reverence to God.

Moses and Elijah (4:4-6)

The final verses of the Book of Malachi are probably a post-script by a pious scribe, seeking to provide a suitable conclusion for the Book of the Twelve (Minor) Prophets as well as for the Book of Malachi. Though the reference to Elijah is appropriately near the beginning of the New Testament in English Bibles, it is only at the end of the second major division of the Hebrew Bible, being followed by the whole collection of "the Writings."

The reader is reminded (4:4) to keep the Law of Moses, commanded at Horeb. The use of the word "Horeb" and the characterization of Moses as "my servant" suggest that it is the Law as recorded in Deuteronomy which is in the mind of the scribe who made the addition (see Deut. 1:6).

Another addition promises that God will send Elijah the prophet before the Day of the Lord. Elijah's mission will be to heal the division between parents and children so that the land will be spared the curse of utter destruction. No reference is made to the cleansing of the Temple of 3:1-4 or to the ethical problems referred to in 3:5, but it seems that the scribe was nevertheless identifying the expected messenger with a returned Elijah. Elijah was chosen in this connection not because he was the earliest of the prophets (Nathan preceded him), or the greatest of them, but because Elijah's unique disappearance from the earth (II Kings 2:11-12) made it appear possible for him to return in connection with the day of divine intervention. It is significant that though the book closes on the terrifying note of divine judgment and destructive intervention, this threat is coupled with the promise that Elijah "will turn the hearts of fathers to their children and the hearts of children to their fathers" in renewed harmony such as God always requires.